MENTAL HEALTH AND W

FOUNDATIONS OF MENTAL HEALTH PRACTICE

The Foundations of Mental Health Practice series offers a fresh approach to the field of mental health by exploring key areas and issues in mental health from a social, psychological and a biological perspective. Taking a multidisciplinary approach, the series is aimed at students and practitioners across the people professions- including student nurses, social workers, occupational therapists, psychiatrists, counsellors and psychologists.

Thurstine Basset worked as a community worker and social worker before becoming involved in mental health training and education in the 1980s. He is an independent training and development consultant and has experience of working with a number of universities, statutory and voluntary mental health organisations, service user and carer groups. He has published widely across the mental health training and education fields. In collaboration with Theo Stickley,he is a Co-editor of 'Learning about Mental Health Practice' (Wiley 2008). He is also a Board Member for the Journal of Mental Health Training, Education and Practice.

Theo Stickley is Associate Professor of Mental Health Nursing at the University of Nottingham. He has authored and edited many books and journal articles about mental health. Each represents. He has authored and edited many books and journal articles about mental health. Each represents his interest in promoting a fair, just and genuinely caring way in which to think about and deliver mental health care. His area of research is promoting mental health through participatory arts and he advocates a creative approach to care delivery.

Available now:

Working with Dual Diagnosis: A Psychosocial Perspective by Darren Hill, William J Penson and Divine Charura

From Psychiatric Patient to Citizen Revisited by Liz Sayce

Models of Mental Health by Gavin Davidson, Jim Campbell, Ciaran Shannon and Ciaran Mulholland

Values and Ethics in Mental Health: An Exploration for Practice by Alastair Morgan, Anne Felton, Bill Fulford, Jaysree Kalathil and Gemma Stacey

Peer Support in Mental Health by Emma Watson and Sara Meddings

MENTAL HEALTH AND WELLBEING

INTERCULTURAL PERSPECTIVES

CHARLES WATTERS

First published 2020 by
RED GLOBE PRESS

Red Globe Press in the UK is an imprint of Springer Nature Limited, registered in England, company number 785998, of 4 Crinan Street, London, N1 9XW.

Red Globe Press® is a registered trademark in the United States, the United Kingdom, Europe and other countries.

ISBN 978–1–137–61022–5 paperback

This book is printed on paper suitable for recycling and made from fully managed and sustained forest sources. Logging, pulping and manufacturing processes are expected to conform to the environmental regulations of the country of origin.

A catalogue record for this book is available from the British Library.

A catalog record for this book is available from the Library of Congress.

Contents

Acknowledgments

I wish to thank academic colleagues across many countries, in particular, the USA, UK, Brazil and Sweden for valuable conversations and insights that have stimulated my thinking while writing this book. There are many, well beyond the space available to me here. I particularly with to mention friends from the Society for Psychological Anthropology including Kristin Yarris, Whitney Duncan and Bridget Haas. I also wish to thank Kristin Yarris for a productive and insightful month spent at the University of Oregon in 2018 that give me opportunities to deepen reflection on many of the themes in the book and their resonance in different country contexts. Earlier visits to Brazil informed my thinking on religion, spirituality and wellbeing and the discussion of ex-voto offerings. I wish to thank friends from the University of Brasilia and the Universidade Católica de Brasília, UCB, who facilitated visits and who have opened many doors including Francisco Martins, Maria Gondim and Marta de Freitas. I wish also to thank colleagues who contributed to summer symposiums offered by the Centre for Innovation and Research on Wellbeing at the University of Sussex including Jo Boyden from the Young Lives Project at the University of Oxford, Jules Pretty from the University of Essex, Dolf te Lintelo from the Institute of Development Studies, Dan Osborn from University College London, Kevin Fenton from Public Health England and Sussex colleagues Tish Marrable, Russell Whiting, Melissa Nolas, Elaine Sharland and David Orr. Particular thanks is due to researchers Emma Soye, Ines Meier and Anna Ridgewell for their significant contributions to research projects and symposia that have deepened debate and thinking in the field. I am also deeply indebted to a network of colleagues across Europe who I have worked with on themes relating to migration and wellbeing over more than two decades including Ilse Derluyn at the University of Ghent, Anders Hjern at University of Stockholm and Ketil Eide from the University of South Eastern Norway. While many have stimulated thinking and debate and offered generous support, errors, omissions and limitations in the text are entirely my responsibility.

A special debt of gratitude is owed to series editor Thurstine Basset for his unflinching support of the project, including the review process and offering consistently insightful comments on the scope of the text. I wish also to thank Peter Hooper and Hannah Watson at Red Globe Press for excellent editorial support throughout the process and Vignesh Viswanathan for skilful management of technical production.

Finally, I wish to thank many members of my family who offered unstinting support; Tamara, who was always a voice of encouragement and practical support; children Joseph, Shane and Dominic and grandchildren Ayva and Leo. Joseph worked tirelessly in helping creating the index while Ayva and Leo offered valuable support in compiling the bibliography.

1

Introduction

Charles Watters

A walk through any city or provincial town in, say, contemporary England, France, the USA or Brazil reveals the impact of heterogeneous ideas and services relating to mental health and wellbeing derived from many parts of the globe: Chinese and Ayurvedic medicine, yoga, reiki, tai chi, chi-kung, mindfulness, various forms of massage, sauna and spa treatments. Some of these practices are relatively recent, for example, the growth of mindfulness, in a secularised form outside of a Buddhist context, can be traced to the 1980s while yoga and tai-chi have been present for several decades more. Some practices were brought as part of a migratory process, for example, Chinese medicine was originally established to serve the needs of the Chinese and South East Asian diaspora just as Ayurvedic and Unani medicine travelled with migrants from Hindu India and the Islamic world. With rapidly accelerated migration and exchanges of ideas, treatments and understandings of the relationship between body and mind from many parts of the globe have become co-present with conventional forms of medicine and, in some notable cases, been incorporated into mainstream health systems.

In the contemporary world it is routine for people in many countries to blend diverse practices drawn from many traditions in seeking wellbeing in their daily lives. It is, for example, unremarkable nowadays for someone to go to morning yoga or meditation before coming to work, or for institutions to offer staff sessions on mindfulness, yoga or tai chi. Despite the fact that these systems and practices are informed by distinctive models of the body and understandings of how mind and body interrelate, in practice people seeking wellbeing navigate seamlessly between them. Models and practices may be derived from different parts of the world: e.g. India, China, Scandinavia, Japan and many are centuries old. While these have originated in specific localities they have, over time, crossed continents and, in doing so, adapted and been informed by new environments and cultural contexts. Adherents of particular practices may have been originally from specific ethnic groups, but as these modalities have travelled they have attracted interest from diverse and heterogeneous populations.

This book examines how models and practices of mental health and wellbeing intersect in an age of migration and mobility. It aims to complement an array of recent books that have offered critical overviews of models and theories of mental health and insights into policy and practice (Davidson et al., 2015 Glasby and Tew, 2015) but is significant not least in looking beyond the Western tradition at the dynamic intercultural influences on models of mental health and wellbeing . It is informed by recognition that we live in an age of unprecedented human movement that, accompanied by the development of digital technologies, has given rise to an extraordinarily rapid exchange of ideas. This environment has a profound impact on mental health and wellbeing giving rise to at least two substantive questions:

How does cultural and ethnic diversity impact on people's mental health and wellbeing?

How is the shape of services and treatments changing in multi-ethnic and multicultural environments?

In addressing these questions the arguments presented in this book challenge notions of boundedness, and national and cultural homogeneity. A brief initial example would be the case of tai-chi, a form of exercise that can be found in many parts of the world including China, Japan,

Europe, North and South America and Australasia. Tai-chi is commonly thought to derive from 13th century Chinese martial arts. However, the roots of tai-chi can be traced further back, to the Tao Te Ching, an ancient Chinese text, from 2,300 to 2,500 years old (Waley, 2013) that emphasises balance between humans and the natural environment as fundamental to wellbeing. The text gave rise to a series of exercises aimed at enhancing bodily and psychological harmony consistent with laws of nature. These exercises are informed by an understanding of nature as consisting of fundamental types of energy, yin and yang. Yin energy is associated with qualities such as femininity, softness, darkness, primordial formlessness while yang is viewed as a male energy associated with dynamism vigour, light and form. For wellbeing, these energies must be brought into balance as imbalance results in poor health; physically, emotionally and psychologically. Tai-chi is a technique that restores and maintains harmony, so that body, mind and emotions become integrated. While rooted in ancient Chinese understandings of the relationship between body, mind and nature, the practice of tai-chi is increasingly recognized in Western countries as having benefits for both mental and physical health. The UK National Health Service (NHS), for example, advises that for tai-chi 'studies have shown that it can help people aged 65 and over to reduce stress, improve posture, balance and general mobility, and increase muscle strength in the legs' (NHS 2019).

While the claims made by the NHS are more circumscribed than those that may be found in traditional Chinese and Japanese medicine, it is notable that an exercise form, derived from very different cultural roots has found a degree of official recognition within one of Europe's largest mainstream health systems. Moreover, the benefits here are identified as both physical and psychological, impacting on both stress and posture, suggesting a holistic perspective on wellbeing. Tai-chi may be seen here an example of the *transitions* that are made between geographical and cultural contexts and also the *transformations* that may take place in practices from one cultural context to another. In further examples, mindfulness practices have transitioned between roots in Buddhist monasticism and to incorporation within various Western medical programmes. In the course of this transition the practice has transformed into a secularised form consistent with the organizational cultures of hospitals, schools and workplaces. Thus here I refer to *transitions* as global movements of ideas and practices relating to mental health and wellbeing and *transformations* as the way these have been adapted in different cultural, social and economic contexts.

The idea of transitions and transformations is fundamental to the use of the term *intercultural* in the book. It is employed here to bring into focus the ways in which cultures impact on each other through processes that result in dynamic cultural change. A central argument is that an understanding of the contemporary landscape of mental health and wellbeing, both in terms of ideas and service developments, is best understood as involving these dual aspects of transitions and transformations. This dynamism is arguably not adequately conveyed by the term 'multicultural' as this may suggest an image of cultures existing alongside each other with little mutual influence. The Nobel Prize winning philosopher and economist Amartya Sen, for example, points to this limitation in referring to multiculturalism as suggesting what he terms 'serial monoculturalism' in which people are seen as existing within fixed cultural worlds with little interpenetration (Sen, 2007). By contrast, the idea of culture employed here echos contemporary anthropological understandings, in which cultures are seen as dynamic and in flux. It thus departs from a view of cultures as 'homogeneous systems, which produce individuals who are culture-bearers and whose behaviour is largely determined by shared cultural models, values and perspectives', towards viewing culture as a process, not a thing, and 'part of, open, fluid, dynamic systems with much internal variation, conflict and contestation' (Kirmayer, 2012 p97).

The term intercultural here also seeks to convey a sense of cultural transitions and transformations as involving the role of agents, including individuals, communities and institutions. There are parallels to the idea, found in historical studies, of 'intercultural transfers' – referring to transitions of cultural products, including artefacts and technologies between countries, and the role of individuals and institutions in giving and receiving countries. The idea of intercultural transitions used here is close to that of cultural diffusion through which behaviour patterns, ideas and artefacts are transmitted within and between locations and generations (Whiten et al., 2016). In the present context the terms intercultural, transitions and transformations are thus used in what may be seen as a nuanced and expanded sense to refer also to transfers between groups who have migrated between countries and processes of cultural appropriation that may be legacies of colonialism and consequently imbued with power relations. The agents here may be people who have migrated, established themselves in a new country and developed new relations with their countries of origin. An example may be those of Indian origin in the UK who may maintain, or may have developed, a wide range of relations of exchange, encompassing ideas and material goods, with the country of origin and perhaps the Indian diaspora elsewhere. It also may encompass examples in which a dominant power simply takes ideas and artefacts from another country or culture and adopts them as their own with scant or no acknowledgement of how they were produced and their place within their original cultural context.

Mental health and wellbeing in an age of migration

A central argument here is that an intercultural perspective is vital at a time of unprecedented human migration and mobility and simultaneously, an historical moment in which there is unparalleled engagement with, and incorporation of, models and practices aimed at enhancing wellbeing and mental health that are derived from very diverse cultural contexts. Indeed, it may be argued that one cannot comprehend or engage fully with current beliefs and practices relating to mental health and wellbeing without deepening one's understanding of the dynamic interpenetration of diverse cultural perspectives and models. In this, the spheres of mental health and wellbeing are consistent with, and present challenges akin to, other areas of development in science and the humanities. Human history is full of examples of migration and cultural borrowing and acquisition across a spectrum that includes art, architecture, language, philosophy, religious traditions and practices, technology, political models and fashion. Ideas of 'the good life' and the components of human wellbeing have also travelled across continents and through centuries with, for example, Aristotle's ideas relating to hedonic and eudemonic happiness still forming a basis for academic research and debate on wellbeing centuries after being first formulated in ancient Greece.

However, while there is a long history of salient ideas and practices traveling across countries and regions, the present age may be seen as distinctive in terms of the breadth and diversity of cultural influences and the rapidity with which they are transmitted and transformed. A factor here is the scale of human migration which, as Castles and Miller have observed, is increasingly globalised with a 'tendency for more and more countries to be crucially affected by migratory movements at the same time' and 'international movements of people growing in volume in all major regions' (Castles and Miller, 2009, pp.10–11). Moreover, the contemporary world is characterised by a 'differentiation of migration', whereby most countries do not have simply one type of immigration but a whole range of types at once, such as labour migration, permanent settlement, and the arrival of refugees and undocumented migrants. The differentiation is also notable in terms of the range of people who migrate, with women increasingly in the vanguard of migratory movements, as well as children, many of whom are undocumented and separated (Ruis-Casares et al., 2012, Watters, 2007)

As people migrate, they have introduced diverse ideas about what constitutes the good life, including views on how to bring up children, appropriate business practices, suitable modes of dress and manners, perspectives on the purpose of life and the moral codes people should live by. In some cases this has challenged practices within receiving societies and they, in turn, have had mixed and often polarised reactions to migrants, some seeing them as bringing benefits not least in terms of economic development, with others seeing them as a drain on limited public funds and taking employment opportunities from the indigenous population. Tides of resentment towards migrants – that are particularly manifest in contemporary times towards asylum seekers, refugees and undocumented migrants – have been evident across the globe with many harrowing accounts of racial abuse and discrimination as well as denial of access to services and jobs (Castles and Miller, 2009).

While migration in general has increased and diversified, forced migration in particular has undergone a comparable range of transformations. The scale and diversification of forced migration is due in no small part to the changing nature of war, in which large scale conflicts involving battles between soldiers of opposing armies has been accompanied by a plethora of 'low intensity conflicts'. These mirror shifting power dynamics in the post-Cold War age, in which conflicts between a relatively small number of 'great powers' and their allies jostling for strategic and material advantage have, in some instances, given way to more fractured forms of conflict. Following military engagements in Iraq, Afghanistan, Libya and other Muslim countries, disparate but often networked groups increasingly resort strategically to civilian targets such as subways, trains, tourist resorts, theatres and airports as evident, for example, from the 9/11 attacks on the World Trade Centre, the 2004 Madrid train bombings, the 2007 subway bombings in London, the attacks at the Bataclan Theatre and the Stade de France in Paris in 2015, the killings of tourists in Tunisia in 2015, and the Brussels Airport and Nice attacks in 2016. The complexities of contemporary conflict are demonstrated in many contexts including the case of Syria where the Assad regime has been supported by an international coalition including Russia and Iran, while opposition forces have been backed by uneasy alliances involving Western powers such as the USA and UK and regional partners including Saudi Arabia and Turkey.

At the time of writing, conflicts in Syria, Iraq and Afghanistan are major driving forces of contemporary forced migration. According to 2018 figures provided by the United Nations High Commission for Refugees, 70.8 million people were forcibly displaced at the end of 2018, the highest figure ever recorded by the agency, a figure roughly equivalent to the total population of the United Kingdom. This figure includes a significant number of internally displaced persons (IDPs) with the number of people uprooted in their own countries growing to an unprecedentedly high number of 41.3 million (UNHCR, 2018). These figures are also exacerbated by a very low proportion of those crossing international borders feeling able to return to their own countries, owing to protracted violence and upheaval. The origin of refugees reflects the changing face of global conflict with over half coming from Syria, Afghanistan and Iraq alone. The broad impacts of displacement are also illustrated in the multiple destinations of refugees showing, for example, that the 4.9 million Syrian refugees are present in no less than 120 receiving countries worldwide. Evidence that all parts of civilian society experience the impact of armed conflicts is provided by breakdown of the population of concern by age and gender, indicating that approximately 48% are women and 51% children under the age of 18 (ibid.). In sum, current trends point to the fact that forced migration is a growing phenomenon in the modern age. It is increasing in terms of the sheer numbers of persons involved, in the types of migrant journeys that are taking place, in the diversity of migrants' nationalities, ethnicities and religions as well as in the diversity of gender and age.

Besides the issue of migration is that of human mobility. While migration relates to movement with the intention to settle (at the very least temporarily) in another country or region, mobility points to the way in which people move around the world without intention to settle and develop networks in different countries and locations. Eisenlohr has, for example, examined the extreme mobility of Muslims in Mauritius, who have developed networks in the UK, USA, India and the Middle East and through business and family ties maintain valued relations across these countries (Eisenlohr, 2012). The anthropologist Thomas Csordas has pointed to the importance of mobility in generating the flow of religious ideas and practices, including perspectives on wellbeing. These may involve the generation of quite specific links between countries and he offers examples in which practices adopted in the West have subsequently led to the development of teachers who have, in some instances, returned to the country where the practice originated. He notes that 'travel between Brazil and the Netherlands resulted in expansion of the Santo Daime church to Europe, the mobility of Korean shamans creates a global reach for their activities, and the ability of American yoga practitioners to relocate to India results in a return globalisation of Hindu practices from their instantiation abroad' (Csordas, 2007, p.262). Contrary to the idea of religion being a manifestation of resistance to globalisation, Csordas has noted the extreme mobility of religions and practices associated with religions. There are numerous examples, from the rise and spread of evangelical churches across the Americas and Europe (a phenomenon that is often linked to migrant populations, for example, Latin American churches such as the Assembly of God, that has found roots in London through the Brazilian population), to Buddhism where different forms of the religion have spread from South East Asia across North America, Europe and Australasia. The practice of mindfulness, rooted in Buddhism, has developed in a secularised form and gained significant traction across the globe entering into mainstream health and social care services across many Western countries. This secularised form of mindfulness practice has been subsequently introduced into Thailand where it forms part of therapeutic hospital programmes (Cassaniti, 2018).

One can discern here a process of 'return migration' for certain cultural practices associated with mental health and wellbeing in which a practice adopted in the West has been transformed, appropriated and then exported to a country of origin. The anthropologist

Cassaniti provides a vivid account of her conversation with a nurse in a psychiatric hospital in Thailand in which the nurse describes the secularised programme of mindfulness they have introduced from the USA. The nurse acknowledges that mindfulness is '*totally* a Buddhist concept' but that she cannot teach it in a Buddhist way, 'because we do the programme from America, and they don't teach it that way. We get our funds from there ... ' (2018, p.5 author's emphasis). In this instance, the practice has transitioned to the West, transformed there and reintroduced to a country of origin in its transformed state.

The diffusion of ideas is also influenced by the exponential growth of digital communications. The latest ITU data estimate that more than half of the world's households (53.6%) by 2016 had access to the Internet at home, compared with less than 20% in 2005 and just over 30% in 2010 (International Telecommunications Union, Geneva 2017). Within the physical context of family households, there is potential to engage with vast global sources of information and networks. However, there is a digital divide in that those in lower income countries have generally more limited access, for example, through low broadband speeds and are more often recipients of internet content rather than its creators. In the sphere of mental health and wellbeing the internet is a powerful tool in disseminating ideas about what it means to live well, about a wide range of therapeutic options people may have for a vast array of conditions. For example, a search on Google using the words 'treatment for depression' gives rise to over 3 million responses, including information of the efficacy of drugs, exercise regimes, cognitive behavioural therapy, electroconvulsive therapy, psychotherapy, mindfulness and many more modalities of treatment. *The Lancet* has reported on research into digital resources for enhancing mental health interventions and identified evaluation evidence in support of 'technology for supporting clinical care and educating health workers, mobile tools for facilitating diagnosis and detection of mental disorders, technologies for promoting treatment adherence and supporting recovery, online self-help programmes for individuals with mental disorders, and programmes for substance misuse prevention and treatment' (Naslund et al., 2017, p.486).

The role of migration, mobilities and digital technologies will be examined further in relation to the diffusion of ideas and practices associated with wellbeing and mental health. Before doing so, it is important to consider the meaning of the central concepts of mental health and wellbeing.

Mental health and wellbeing: conceptual and theoretical orientations

From the outset, it is important to note the ways in which the concepts of mental health and wellbeing are interrelated. A helpful starting point is the definition offered by Dudley et al. in their volume *Mental Health and Human Rights*, and it may be worth quoting at length:

> We take 'mental health' to refer to diverse activities directly or indirectly related to the mental well-being component of the World Health Organization (WHO)'s definition of health; 'A state of complete physical, mental and social well-being, and not merely the absence of disease.' While recognising that common and historical usage tends to equate 'mental health' with professionals and services associated with the diagnosis, treatment and rehabilitation of people affected by

mental disorders, mental health also encompasses the promotion of well-being, the prevention of mental disorders ... and the right to the highest attainable standard of physical and mental health.

The authors go on to argue that from a wider perspective, mental health incorporates all the dimensions of human experience: 'biological, psychological, socio-cultural, developmental, political, ecological and spiritual', while noting that a subject of scientific investigation and empirical study is 'also a social construct insofar as different cultures and social groups shape how it is understood and how mental health disturbances arise and are remedied (Dudley et al., 2012, p.3). The interrelationship between the concepts of mental health and wellbeing are apparent here on a number of levels. Mental health is related explicitly by the WHO to a view of health as complete physical, mental and social wellbeing, and incorporates bodies, minds and social relations. Also the scope of mental health is not only the eradication, amelioration and prevention of mental disorders but more proactively and positively a state of complete wellbeing.

This definition offers a more comprehensive and widely interdisciplinary orientation to mental health than found within professional perspectives offered by various mental health disciplines such as psychology, psychiatry and psychotherapy (Rose, 2018). It indicates an integrated and holistic view incorporating multiple dimensions of human existence from the physical to the psychological, emotional and spiritual. Within this, mental health is recognised here as culturally and socially constructed in terms of parameters of mental health and illness, and the aetiologies and treatments of mental health problems. While there are strong linkages here between mental health and wellbeing, the latter concept is not defined in the above definition beyond suggesting the interrelationship between physical, mental and social dimensions. A useful starting point for further exploration of the concept of wellbeing is consideration of Aristotle's reflections on hedonic and eudemonic happiness, that have informed academic and professional discussion and debate over the centuries.

Put briefly, hedonic concepts of happiness emphasise the maximization of pleasure and of relief from pain. So, to be happy, we must seek and realise experiences and sensations that we find pleasurable and enjoyable while eradicating or, at least reducing, those that give us pain. By contrast, a eudemonic concept views happiness as not merely a pursuit of pleasure, at least in a narrow physiological desire driven sense, but rather as a deeply satisfying state that is derived from acting in accordance with virtue; from an aspiration towards the good. Aristotle offers the following definition of a 'happy man'; 'one who is active in accordance with complete virtue, and who is adequately furnished with external goods, and that not for some unspecified period but throughout a complete life' (2004, p.24). Virtue in turn is defined as consisting of two classes: intellectual and moral. Intellectual virtues include wisdom, understanding and prudence, while liberality and temperance are classed as moral virtues. Intellectual virtue can be taught over time and through experience while moral virtue is a product of habit (2004, p.31). According to Aristotle, 'wisdom is admittedly the most pleasant of the virtuous activities ... the wise man, no less than the just one and all the rest, requires the necessities of life, but given an adequate supply of these, the just man also needs people with and towards whom he can perform just actions ... ' (Aristotle, 2004, p.270). There are two particularly important points here that are reflected in contemporary studies of wellbeing. One is that a certain level of necessities, or of material wellbeing in contemporary language, is required to support the realisation of higher aspirations. However, it is suggested here that once these necessities are present, there is little pleasure to be gained in terms of eudemonic happiness by subsequent accumulation. This has been reflected in contemporary studies of wellbeing in which it has been observed that a certain level of material resource is necessary to experience more general wellbeing, but further accumulation does not, in itself, increase happiness (Belton, 2014). A second point is that eudemonic happiness may be realised through engagement with others. One's own qualities take on tangible form through interactions that are directed by these qualities. So, in an example offered by Aristotle, a just man experiences his virtue of justice through exercising justice on others. Human society becomes the forum for developing and realising substantial happiness in the sense of action in accordance with virtue. While stressing relational aspects, Aristotle does also refer to a higher pleasure that may be derived from contemplation but while this may be a solitary activity, is also achieved 'better with the help of fellow-workers' (2004, p.271).

Echoes of Aristotelian thought are found in contemporary formulations of the dimensions of human wellbeing. These consistently stress as core elements a physical or material dimension, psychological or subjective wellbeing and social or relational wellbeing. Each of these dimensions is seen as interrelated and mutually reinforcing. Psychological and social wellbeing rests on having an adequate level of material resources (this can be variously defined in different cultural contexts), and on having good, trusting relations with others, which enhances psychological wellbeing that in turn opens greater potential for developing relationships. In a recent formulation of wellbeing, Fischer has identified three core components: adequate material resources, physical health and safety, and family and social relations, and adds what he describes as three more subjective domains: aspiration and opportunity, dignity and fairness, and commitment to a larger purpose (Fischer, 2014, p.5). Turning back to consider the WHO definition of mental health as 'a state of complete physical, mental and social well-being, and not merely the absence of disease', one can see that formulations of wellbeing encompass at the very least, these dimensions of the physical, psychological and relational.

The closeness between concepts of mental health and wellbeing can be recognised in further contemporary formulations. The following conceptualisation of mental health is offered in the context of the World Health Organisation 2013–20 Mental Health Action Plan: 'a state of wellbeing in which the individual realizes his or her own abilities, can cope with the normal stresses of life, can work productively and fruitfully, and is able to make a contribution to his or her community' (WHO, 2013). This conceptualisation is close to that frequently offered for 'subjective wellbeing' (SWB) and has been used to describe a state of satisfaction with life and emotional equilibrium. According to a survey of the field by Keyes, 'definitions and research on subjective wellbeing were initially oriented towards a hedonic conceptualisation...a specific dimension of subjective well-being that consists of perceptions of avowed interest in life, happiness and satisfaction with life, and the balance of positive to negative affect. In contrast, 'eudaimonic well-being, sometimes referred to as positive functioning, consists of individual's evaluation of their psychological well-being' (Keyes, 2006, p.4). The framing of eudemonic wellbeing was, as such, significantly broader and deeper than the more circumscribed orientation of a hedonic perspective. This breadth was reflected in psychometric measures developed by Ryff and Keyes as encompassing six dimensions: positive evaluation of oneself and one's past life, a sense of continued growth and development as a person, the belief that one's life is purposeful and meaningful, the possession of quality relations with others, the capacity to manage effectively one's life and surrounding world, and a sense of self-determination (Ryff and Keyes, 1995). White and colleagues have argued that high levels of eudaimonia have been linked to people having an increased purpose in life, and greater levels of social integration, personal growth, social contribution, and autonomy. 'Flourishing' has been introduced as a term to describe individuals with high levels of emotional, psychological and social wellbeing, and the term 'languishing' is used to describe individuals who are experiencing low levels of emotional, psychological and social wellbeing (White, S., & Abeyasekera, A. 2014, p.2).

Structure of the book

The book is divided into seven chapters including an introduction and conclusion. Part 1 focusses on exploring perspectives on migration and mobility in mental health and wellbeing, encompassing movement and networking involving both physical travel and digital space. It offers a reflection on the implications of both the rapid movements of people and of ideas for the shaping of contemporary view and practices. It consists of a chapter on migration, mobility and cultural diversity that examines three influential theoretical frameworks for understanding the impacts of migration and cultural diversity. These are social capital, acculturation theory and the capabilities approach. We examine specifically the implications and potential these approaches have for understanding the mental health and wellbeing of different cultural groups. The chapter also offers a critical reflection on the idea of the ethnic or cultural 'group' in research, service design and development and suggests ways forward that offers a more central place to peoples own understandings of their cultures and groups. The second chapter of Part 1 is focussed on exploring religion and spirituality in relation to mental health and wellbeing. It includes consideration of distinctions between ideas of 'religion' and 'spirituality' and how these may reflect socially or personally oriented ideals and practices. We explore the place of religion and spirituality in the quest for healing and the ways in which different models of body and mind (offered by Chinese medicine for example) have been integrated into health care systems.

The second part of the book is more specifically oriented towards examining services and the ideas that underpin them in culturally diverse settings. This includes exploring perspectives on assimilation, multiculturalism and anti-racism and how these influence the way social challenges are perceived and responded to. This part of the book includes a chapter on the place of nature in wellbeing and mental health, and examines how ideas of nature from different traditions and parts of the world are proving influential. It includes consideration of the healing potential of nature, and explores the impact of engagement with the natural environment on wellbeing. Consideration is given to some of the barriers that may influence engagement including the way natural environments may be promoted as the preserve of more elite groups in societies. The third chapter in the second part of the book examines the way mental health and wellbeing services are being reshaped through intercultural influences such as through the dynamic rise of mindfulness practices and their impact across a spectrum of environments including health care services, education and the workplace.

The rise of Open Dialogue is also considered here, and how, from its origins in Finland, it has come to play an increasingly influential role in mental health care in the UK and in other European countries. We also consider practices that are influential but outside the mainstream including shamanism and family constellations.

The book concludes with a reflection on the potential for the development of integrative approaches to mental health and wellbeing that are informed by intercultural perspectives. We note in particular the rise of social prescribing, an approach increasingly influential in the UK and that offers the potential for a wide range of practices, including engagement with nature, cookery, museum visits, mindfulness, yoga and tai-chi to be incorporated into a prescribed programme of activities aimed at enhancing mental health and wellbeing.

Part 1

PERSPECTIVES ON MIGRATION AND MOBILITY IN MENTAL HEALTH AND WELLBEING

2

Migration, Mobility and Cultural Diversity: Implications for Mental Health and Wellbeing

Chapter Overview

- Mental health and wellbeing should be seen in the context of the 'Age of Migration' in which dynamic changes to populations are taking place. Those who migrate are increasingly diverse in terms of social class, gender, ethnicity and cultural backgrounds.

- Migration includes both people who cross international borders and those who are internal migrants, many of whom move from rural to urban areas in the hope of enhancing their economic wellbeing.

- Migration is often accompanied by enhanced social pressures, with newcomers viewed as a threat to the livelihood and wellbeing of host populations. Host societies are often sharply polarised between those who welcome migrants and those who see them as a threat to social stability.

- While the building of social capital enhances mental health and wellbeing, an influential perspective from the social capital literature views people as 'hunkering down' into their own communities when faced by increasing diversity. This perspective has been challenged by research on contact theory that points to the positive benefits of diversity.

- Research on acculturation points to the benefits of 'integration' – understood as the maintenance of cultural traditions and identities alongside positive social engagement with the host society. Integration is associated with better psychological adaptation.

- The capabilities approach is a fruitful way of developing and evaluating the impact of services and interventions in terms of enhancing mental health and wellbeing.

The late 20th and early 21st century has witnessed a remarkable growth in the extent and diversity of international migration. The pattern has changed from significant migration from one country to a particular destination – from example, the large-scale movement of populations in the mid-20th century from former colonies of European powers such as India and Algeria to the UK and France – to more diverse forms of migration not readily explicable in terms of colonial histories. Part of this phenomenon is, of course, the result of a more globalised economy, or what Castells terms the 'network society' linking the production of goods and services to an ever-expanding interdependent global economy (Castells, 2000). Investments in certain localities generate spaces of concentrated labour migration, production, distribution, exchange and consumption that can be severely disrupted by fluctuations in the global market (Harvey, 2005). A global company such as Apple, for example, with headquarters in California, has had a dramatic impact on patterns of internal migration in China where, as Pun and Chan note, 'successive generations of rural migrant workers have become the mainstay of the country's export-processing sector' (2013, p.179). A key issue here is the interdependence of modes of capitalist production and the movement of people. As geopolitical environments change, companies seek safer and more lucrative environments for production and distribution and the development of services, including financial services. The presence of valued resources and the movement of capital can produce new opportunities for migrants and attract people from across the globe to particular destinations.

Castles and Miller have described our present era as 'The Age of Migration' (2009). This is not to deny there have been significant and dramatic waves of migration throughout history, but rather to suggest that present day migration is unique in both its scale and complexity. Some of these features have been introduced above, and it is appropriate to offer a little more elaboration here as each has a bearing on issues of mental health and wellbeing. Castles and Miller indicate distinctive features of the present age. Firstly they argue that migration is now globalised. As noted, this is manifest in the fact that more and more countries are affected by migratory movements at the same time. They also point out that immigration countries tend to receive migrants from a larger number of source countries, 'so that most countries of immigration have entrants from a broad spectrum of economic, social and cultural backgrounds' (2009, p.10). Alongside this, they note that migration is growing in volume at present. This observation is strongly supported by statistical evidence and indeed the acceleration of migration has been even more evident in recent times.

The International Office for Migration reports that in 2015 there were over one billion migrants in the world, more than one in seven of the world population. Of these, 244 million were international migrants, that is, people who are living outside their countries of birth, while an estimated 740 million were internal migrants, often people who had migrated from rural to urban areas. This included 150 million people who had migrated from the countryside to cities in China. International migrants are concentrated in certain countries of destination, with no less than 51% of all international migrants settled in just ten countries. The USA tops this list with 46.6 million residing there in 2015. Of European countries, Germany had the most foreign-born residents, with some 12 million, followed by the UK with 8.5 million. These movements have resulted in cities being particularly diversified. For example, 37% of the population of London was born outside of the UK, the highest proportion in Europe (IOM, 2018).

The numerical scale of migration coupled with the diversity of countries from which people are migrating has resulted in what some commentators have described as the 'hyper diversity' or 'super diversity' of some countries and urban areas. Meissnet and Vertovec have described super diversity in terms of changing population configurations arising from global migration flows, arguing that 'the changing configurations not only entail the movement of people from more varied national, ethnic, linguistic and religious backgrounds, but also the ways that shifts concerning these categories or attributes coincide with a worldwide diversification of movement flows through specific migration channels (such as work permit programmes, mobilities created by EU enlargement, ever-changing refugee and "mixed migration" flows, undocumented movements, student migration, family reunion, and so on); the changing compositions of various migration channels themselves entail ongoing differentiations of legal statuses (conditions, rights and restrictions), diverging patterns of gender and age, and variance in migrants' human capital (education, work skills and experience)' (Meissner and Vertovec, 2015, p.514).

A feature of the contemporary world is thus the highly differentiated and complex forms of migration. There are more people on the move, from a greater variety of countries. But there is also considerable variation in the statuses of migrants, and this has profound implications for mental health and wellbeing. There are, as Meissner and Vertovec note, a diversification of migration channels (what I have previously described as 'avenues of access', Watters, 2001) and these link to differing legal statuses with concomitant rights and restrictions. For example, a sought-after academic or software engineer, may gain access to the USA as a 'person of exceptional ability'. Her visa allows her to work and live in the US and, like US citizens and permanent residents, to pay taxes. However, there are also restrictions with this status. Residence is temporary, perhaps for a period of three years before which application for another visa has to be made, and during the time of residence the visa holder has limited rights to welfare and political participation. For those entering countries with even more precarious statuses, for example, as asylum seekers and undocumented migrants, there are substantially more restrictions in terms of access to support and services. As we shall see, asylum seekers may have very limited access to only emergency health services while undocumented migrants may have no access to health or welfare support. Thus, the general point here is that, migratory status affects entitlements and this has a powerful effect in terms of the physical, emotional and psychological experience of migration and the access to health and mental health services migrants may have. Before examining implications for mental health and wellbeing, it is important to further identify key features of migration.

Migration: the dynamics of belongingness and otherness

The California gold rush may be a helpful illustrative historical example of salient issues in migration. After gold was discovered in 1848 'everything about California would change. In one astonishing year the place would be transformed from obscurity to world prominence...from a society of neighbours and families to one of strangers and transients' (Holliday, 2015, p.26). During this year the population climbed from around 400 to 90,000. The discovery of gold followed California's incorporation into the United States of America, offering unlimited opportunities for people to travel west from more prosperous and populated states in pursuit of their fortune. There are significant parallels here with contemporary examples of economic migration. In present-day California, Silicon Valley houses the head-quarters of some of the largest global technological companies, it has become a magnet for highly skilled workers from across the globe, with notable numbers of arrivals from the Indian sub-continent and South East Asia, as well as internal migrants from across the USA. The geopolitical changes that arose from the gold rush also suggest parallels with the dynamics of migration in Western Europe. In the past 20 years there has been significant migration to the more prosperous regions of the European Union from those with fewer opportunities. The UK, for example, has enjoyed relatively low rates of unemployment since the turn of the present century and this has been a 'pull' factor for people in many parts of Europe with limited or no job opportunities. At the time of writing, geopolitical factors are however putting severe strain on the free movement of people across Europe, including the closure of borders in response to unprecedented flows of refugees from Syria, Afghanistan, the Horn of Africa and other troubled regions of the world. Further impact on migration is being felt as a result of the UK's likely departure from the European Union. This has deterred some EU migrants from moving to the UK and led to others leaving the UK, resulting in labour shortages in vital services such as the NHS, and in agriculture. In some instances, it has had an opposite effect, leading to an escalation of migration into the UK by those who have initially settled in other EU countries and who have put forward plans to move before formal departure from the EU.

The example of the gold rush is also illustrative in pointing to the way communities can quickly change as a consequence of migration. The arrival of 'transients and strangers' may be accompanied by a polarizing of attitudes towards new arrivals, with some welcoming them as indicative of economic vitality and an opportunity to embrace new cultural forms, and others viewing them with suspicion and seeing them as a threat to community cohesion. These polarizing attitudes are very much a feature of contemporary migration, with significant implications for mental health and wellbeing. The arrival of Syrian refugees in Germany provides a good example of this. Many Germans felt considerable sympathy for the plight of the refugees and arranged warm receptions for them as they arrived by train and bus, with cheering, handshakes, gifts (including children's toys) and offers of support and hospitality. Others saw the economic advantages of this new influx of migrants. Germany has a relatively strong economy but a 'demographic deficit' in terms of a declining adult-age population. Syrian migrants were generally well-educated and of an age to address this deficit, and with children who could, in the course of time, help sustain economic progress. Against these pragmatic and positive views, others saw this as a foolhardy enterprise and argued that the scale of migration was too great to be absorbed without disrupting communities and generating a range of social problems. Moreover, this largely Muslim population was depicted as having values that were fundamentally at variance with that of the host society, including in relation to attitudes to women, same-sex relationships, Western dress codes and free speech.

An incident at Cologne Station in which asylum-seeking men were identified as harassing German women at a New Year carnival was seen by those opposing immigration as illustrative of the problems the country was now facing. In 2017 the BBC reported: 'Victims have described chaos outside the city's main station, as the men carried out dozens of attacks with little apparent response from the authorities. Correspondents say the identification of the attackers as North African or Arab in appearance caused alarm in Germany because of the influx of more than a million migrants and refugees in the past year' (BBC,

2018). Anti-immigrant sentiment resulted in numerous incidents in which migrants have been attacked, including arson attacks on centres housing asylum seekers. According to the BBC, 'nearly 10 attacks were made on migrants in Germany every day in 2016, the interior ministry says. A total of 560 people were injured in the violence, including 43 children. Three-quarters of the attacks targeted migrants outside of their accommodation, while nearly 1,000 attacks were on housing. Chancellor Angela Merkel's decision to open up Germany to people fleeing conflict and persecution has polarised opinion and been followed by an increase in hate crime' (ibid, 2018).

Migration, mobility and social capital

It is not difficult to see the potential implications of relations between migrants and host societies in terms of mental health and wellbeing. The examples given above identify instances in which wellbeing is threatened in fundamental ways, including what Fischer described (see above) as a core component of wellbeing: 'physical health and safety'. Migrants, in many contemporary contexts, are viewed by a significant proportion of the host society as having ways of life, attitudes and values that are incompatible with those receiving them. The incidents in Cologne reinforce these views, while for the migrants seeking asylum, the attacks on them produce a sense that they are unwelcome and despised by members of the host society. The view of migrants, as a potential threat to social cohesion, is hardly new. From ancient times city-states have been wary of the spectre of the 'uncivilised other' or 'barbarians at the gates' penetrating city walls. Nationalist, anti-immigrant politicians have compared the arrival of refugees as a sort of modern-day Trojan Horse that, after entry to a country, pose a threat from within including their emergence of potential terrorists (Watters 2007).

The idea of the incompatibility of migrants – particularly those from the Muslim world to the West – has been lent intellectual weight by Samuel Huntington's influential and controversial essay entitled the 'Clash of Civilisations?', in which he argued that 'the fundamental source of conflict in the new world will not be primarily ideological or primarily economic. The great divisions among humankind and the dominating source of conflict will be cultural' (1993, p.22). Huntington proposed there were seven, possibly eight civilisations in the contemporary world and that membership of a civilisation was the 'highest cultural grouping of people and the broadest level of cultural identity people have short of that which distinguishes humans from other species'. He went on to predict that the most important conflicts of the future will occur along cultural fault lines that separate civilisations from one another. In listing the reasons for this, he argued that 'the interactions between peoples of different civilizations are increasing; these increasing interactions intensify civilization consciousness and awareness of differences between civilizations and commonalities within civilizations' (ibid., 1993, p.25). He proposed that this is reflected in the hostility felt by French people towards North Africans and the discomfort Americans feel about Japanese investment in their country.

Huntington's essay has been roundly criticised, not least by Edward Said, who witheringly described it in terms of a 'clash of ignorance', not least for a simplistic construction of incompatible and homogeneous civilisations (Said, 2001). However, despite the limitations of its conceptual framework and hypothesis, the ideas underpinning the essay have continuing resonance and inform contemporary political discourse and policy-making. At the time of writing, the idea of the incompatibility of Western and Muslim 'civilisations' is being expressed by controversial and widely publicised comments on the burka made by the former British Foreign Secretary Boris Johnson (The Times, August 18th 2018), that have been likened to Enoch Powell's notorious 'rivers of blood speech' on immigration to the UK (The Guardian, 18th August 2018). US President Donald Trump routinely espouses views on the incompatibility of Muslim and Western values that have materialised in policies aimed at reducing immigration from certain selected Islamic countries. The idea of fundamental incompatibility between the cultures of migrants and those of the host societies offers a bleak vision of community cohesion and adds fuel to arguments against immigration, particularly from Muslims. It suggests that poor relational wellbeing will be a core feature of interethnic relations and that ethnically and culturally heterogeneous cities will become increasingly segregated.

In examining the quality of relational wellbeing and its implications for mental health in culturally diverse contexts, one helpful theoretical lens is offered by social capital. While a number of influential academics have contributed to developing concepts of social capital, including Bourdieu, Coleman, Portes and Fukuyama (Bourdieu, 1986, Coleman, 1988, Portes, 1998, Fukuyama, 2001) the work of the American political scientist, Robert Putnam has been particularly influential in the domains of social policy and service provision. His analysis has profound implications for understanding the factors that lead towards enhancing relational wellbeing within contexts of ethnic diversity and cultural complexity. Putnam's 2001 book, *Bowling Alone: The collapse and revival of American community*, drew its inspiration from the observation that more and more Americans were going to bowling alleys alone rather than with family and friends (Putnam, 2001). Bowling has been seen as a quintessentially community-oriented activity, and the phenomenon of more and more people bowling alone is taken as a metaphor for the decline of the American community. Putnam goes on to examine evidence for a decline in community, noting, for example, less involvement in political groups and organisations and engagement in community and neighbourhood groups. While Bourdieu was concerned with examining social capital in order to understand processes of social reproduction and social inequality, Putnam has had a more practical focus. He defined social capital in terms of 'connections among individuals – social networks and the norms of reciprocity and trustworthiness that arise from them' (Putnam, 2001, p.19). A central issue for Putnam is examining the bonds of trust that exist between people, how these have been eroded and how they can be rebuilt. High levels of social capital are equated with positive social outcomes including educational success, good health (including good mental health), low crime and harmonious community living. Consistent with Putnam, the Organisation for Economic Co-operation and Development (OECD) defines social capital as 'networks together with shared norms, values and understandings that facilitate cooperation within or among groups' (Keeley, 2007, p.102). The OECD elaborates that the concept consists of three components, as follows:

Bonds: Links to people based on a sense of common identity ('people like us') – such as family, close friends and people who share our culture or ethnicity.

Bridges: Links that stretch beyond a shared sense of identity, for example to distant friends, colleagues and associates.

Linkages: Links to people or groups further up or lower down the social ladder. www.oecd.org/insights/37966934.pdf (accessed 11th August 2018).

In terms of considering human wellbeing, social capital may be seen as a way of unpacking an idea of relational wellbeing through emphasising the role of networks, bonds and bridges between people. The key elements of social capital, usually identified as the elements of 'bonding' and 'bridging', can be seen as operating on two levels. According to Almedom, 'each type of social capital has cognitive and/or structural component(s) and may operate at micro and/or macro level(s). At a micro level, bonding social capital can relate to shared values and mutual trust felt by individuals, families and households, while bridging social capital can relate more widely, at macro levels, to links between voluntary and community groups and vertically between groups and statutory and non-statutory bodies. Effective mental health policy and service provision may build or strengthen bridging social capital and benefit from both bonding and bridging social capital where either or both exist' (Almedom, 2005, p.943).

The basic idea that good quality human relationships enhance mental health is hardly new in the field. Brown and Harris noted in the 1970s the linkages between an absence of trusting social networks and the presence of depression (Brown and Harris, 2012). Their findings have been supported by subsequent research that highlighted the importance of a lack of 'confiding relationships' (one of Brown and Harris' four 'vulnerability factors') as a factor in the presence of depression and a clear risk factor in its development (Patton et al, 2003). Several studies have shown that social capital is associated with mental health outcomes but the precise nature of the relationship has been far from clear. Moreover, there are questions as to whether the impact of social capital on mental health may be different in specific cultural contexts. For example, in a study of mental health and social capital in Columbia, involving over 1168 youths (aged between 15 and 25) it was concluded that; 'When violence factors were added to the model, the "trust" factor fell out and the most important risk factors became (in descending order of importance): being female; no schooling/incomplete primary; and being a victim of violence … the dominance of poverty related factors, as opposed to social capital, prompts renewed attention to the explanatory mechanisms that link income inequality and poor mental health' (Harpham et al., 2004, p.2267). The question of income inequality has been raised more widely in influential studies by Wilkinson and Prickett who have argued from extensive international data that wide inequalities in societies produce a range of social ills including higher crime rates, lower trust and poorer health outcomes including poor mental health (Wilkinson and Pickett, 2010).

There is, as such, considerable debate on the value of a focus on social capital and whether it offers a more helpful explanatory model than one that centres on the relationships between mental health and social inequalities. These debates are underpinned by a recognition of the difficulties in defining both social capital and mental health. As Almedom notes, 'health is conceptually ambiguous and defiant of objective definition, quantification and bureaucratic appropriation, and therefore any measurable associations between social capital and mental health can only be approximate' (Almedom, 2005, p.948). The impact of social capital on mental health is arguably most distinctive at a micro level within the family. Catherine Rothon and colleagues, in a study of family social support, community social capital and adolescent mental health and educational outcomes, noted that, 'In the case of mental health, family social support was particularly pertinent' (Rothon et al., 2012, p.709). Their findings indicated that having a poor relationship with one's parents was associated with higher odds of having mental health problems. Factors such as having regular meals with family members and greater parental surveillance were positive factors. In this context, social class appeared not to be a significant factor nor was the wider context of the quality of community social capital.

The idea of bolstering existing family and community relationships to build social capital receives further support in reviews of evidence of links between social capital and mental health. The former head of the WHO Mental Health Division Norman Sartorius has suggested a two-way process whereby efficient and effective mental health services help to build and/or strengthen social capital in the communities they serve, and are in turn built and strengthened by the social capital of service users (Almedom, 2005; Sartorius, 2003). When one considers this challenge in the context of ethnic and cultural diversity, a key issue is the building of bridging social capital. How do you nurture the development of social capital among communities with differing cultural values, or are we moving, as Huntington suggested, towards an inevitable clash of civilisations?

Pessimistic views of the potential for harmonious living in contexts of cultural diversity are widespread in academic literature and in contemporary political discourses. Putnam has added to that sense of pessimism by arguing that evidence from research into social capital indicates that people tend to absorb themselves into their own communities in contexts of diversity, suggesting, at first glance, stronger 'bonding' social capital and more limited 'bridging'. However, he goes even further and suggests that not only do people recoil from outgroups in contexts of diversity, they even 'hunker down' from people in their own groups, rather like a tortoise pulls into its shell. Putnam's conclusions were reached on the basis of a large general population sample in the USA (the Social Capital Community Benchmark Study, 2007 see Putnam 2007). He concluded that individuals residing in areas characterised by greater ethnic diversity reported not only lower levels of outgroup trust, but also of neighbourhood trust (i.e., trust of one's neighbours), and even ingroup trust. The image evoked by Putman was one of mistrustful and atomised individuals and communities, of people feeling threatened by diversity and disengaging from the world. Within the UK, the former head of the Commission for Equalities and Human Rights, Trevor Phillips, evoked a complementary vision arguing that Britain is 'sleepwalking to segregation' as communities increasingly turn in on themselves (Phillips, 2005).

However, this perspective has been challenged on the basis of a meta-analysis of international studies, demonstrating that the evidence supporting Putnam's view is mixed and most studies suggesting negative effects from diversity are based on data from the United States (Hewstone et al 2015, p.419). Hewstone and colleagues argue instead for understanding intergroup relations through contact theory; that engaging in positive contact with individuals from different groups promotes positive intergroup attitudes. According to Hewstone, 'while Putnam argues that, at least in the short term, diversity has a negative impact, from contact theory I argue that diverse contexts offer opportunities for positive intergroup contact, i.e. for having positive face-to-face interactions with those diverse others who make up one's social environment. Therefore, individuals living in geographical units with greater proportional shares of outgroup residents tend to have more intergroup contact. There is, then, empirical evidence that intergroup contact tends to exert positive effects on intergroup attitudes, reduced intergroup threat perceptions, and trust' (Hewstone 2015, p.420).

I have argued elsewhere that there is further evidence that Putnam's view is not supported by examining the situation in the UK. Here, as demographers Finney and Simpson have noted, communities and ethnic groups are becoming more integrated and there is also significant evidence of upward social mobility among members of black and minority ethnic (BAME) groups. While issues of migration and integration have been the focus of policy debate and academic research across the globe, they have assumed a distinctive pattern within the UK. In general, academic responses to the situation in the UK have been negative and focused on a perceived prevalence of racist attitudes in the general population and embedded in institutions. In this context, Adrian Favell has noted the prevalence and distinctive features of a British 'anti-racism' that pervades academic and public policy-making (Favell, 2001). Indeed, academics outside the UK often assume that the preoccupation with racism in British scholarship arises because of the particular depth and ubiquity of the problem in British society. Within this context, it is not difficult to see why the post-9/11 and post-7/7 attack on British multiculturalism met with little resistance among scholars (for notable exceptions, see Meer and Modood, 2009). After all, if racist attitudes and practices remain deeply embedded in British society, does this not support the thesis that the multiculturalist programmes have indeed failed?

Exercise 2.1

Consider the extent to which social capital may enhance the mental health or wellbeing of a specific cultural group. What may be the specific challenges in enhancing bonding and bridging social capital? What steps may those offering mental health or social support services take to help develop social capital?

The problem with much theorizing around race and ethnicity is a growing gap between what Favell identifies as British 'anti-racism' (2001) and evidence from contemporary empirical studies. As noted, recent findings have pointed to closer demographic integration of ethnic groups, a comparatively high level of mixed marriages and relationships, improving social attitudes to diversity, marked improvements in school performance of some ethnic groups and distinctive upward social mobility of some black and minority ethnic (BAME) groups. An international survey undertaken by Ipsos-Mori in 2017 pointed to improving attitudes towards immigration in the UK, with the country identified as having the most pro-immigration attidues in Europe. According to its most recent findings, 'The UK leads the world in being most positive about immigration' (Ipsos-Mori, 2019). Within this context, Finney and Simpson offers a robust challenge to those who paint a bleak picture of race and ethnic relations in contemporary Britain. Contrary to the declaration by Trevor Phillips, the authors contend that Britain is not 'sleepwalking to segregation', and that demographic evidence suggests that precisely the opposite may be happening, with people from different ethnic heritages living ever more closely together and developing stronger ties with each other. Finney and Simpson's findings are remarkable not least for the wealth of data presented but also because they call into question the motivations of those who present Britain's policies on black and minority ethnic (BAME) groups as 'failing'. Their view is also underpinned by studies undertaken by the Institute of Public Policy Research (IPPR), indicating that members of a number of black and minority ethnic (BAME) groups are doing better in areas such as income, education and employment than their white English counterparts (Kyambi, 2005; IPPR, 2007). Moreover, there is evidence over the past decade of large numbers of black and minority ethnic (BAME) groups choosing to leave other European Union countries such as Denmark, the Netherlands and Sweden, and settle instead in the UK, and of tens of thousands of migrants from refugee-producing countries such as Iraq, Afghanistan and Somalia trying desperately to reach Britain from continental Europe via ports on mainland Europe, including Calais, Zeebrugge and Ostend (Derluyn et al., 2012, Watters, 2007).

These examples add emphasis to the broader point that there is insufficient evidence to link diversity to poor social outcomes. The image of communities hunkering down and turning in on themselves presents a bleak picture of mental health and wellbeing in contexts of diversity. However, work orientated around testing the contact hypothesis points towards growing empirical evidence that, where interconnections are present, people from different ethnic and cultural heritages can live together relatively harmoniously. Moreover, population movements from Nordic countries and the Netherlands to the UK challenge the idea that forced migrants arriving in high income countries are seeking to simply live off the largesse of the receiving countries through receiving unemployment benefits and supported housing. If this was the case, why would thousands seek dangerous passage from France or Belgium, or secondary migration from Nordic countries to the UK? The benefits offered in the UK are not better, indeed they are often poorer, than those offered in countries migrants are risking their lives to leave. I will argue that this points to is the importance of seeing migration, even forced migration, in terms of the pursuit of wellbeing, in the sense of a fulfilled life. In this context, Aristotelian distinctions between hedonic and eudemonic happiness are helpful in that they point to a central notion of happiness being related to a realisation of aspiration and potential beyond the hedonic notion of the maximising of feeling of pleasure.

Acculturation and wellbeing

If there are indeed contexts in which diversity is accompanied by substantive bridging social capital, and the latter is associated with improved mental health and wellbeing, what are the factors that support its development? One helpful area of research in this context is in the field of acculturation. This approach is described by one leading researcher as follows, 'Acculturation is the dual process of cultural and psychological change that takes place as a result of contact between two or more cultural groups and their individual members. At the group level, it involves changes in social structures and institutions and in cultural practices. At the individual level, it involves changes in a person's behavioral repertoire'. These processes of change are highly variable and extend over time, sometimes over centuries: 'there are large group and individual differences in the ways in which people seek to go about their acculturation (termed acculturation strategies), and in the degree to which they achieve satisfactory adaptations. In addition to cultural group and individual variation, there are variations within families: among family members, acculturation often proceeds at different rates, and with different goals, sometimes leading to an increase in conflict and stress and to more difficult adaptations' (Berry, 2005, p.697). A central issue here is that modes of acculturation have significant impacts on mental health and wellbeing.

The Canadian social psychologist John Berry, a leading academic in acculturation research, has argued that there is a spectrum of responses to contact between two or more cultural groups. At one end of the spectrum is cultural maintenance, where groups and individuals seek to ensure the integrity and continuity of cultural modalities, including language, customs, beliefs and values. At the other end of the spectrum is desire for inter-group contact, a reaching out and engagement with the other cultural group or groups. Berry argues that, along this spectrum, people can be seen as adopting one of four acculturation strategies: assimilation, integration, separation or marginalisation. Assimilation relates to circumstances in which individuals do not wish to maintain their cultural identity and seek daily interaction with other cultures. This, as with the other acculturation strategies he proposes, can be seen at a level of individual, family and/community choice but also at the level of law and policy where a government may seek to encourage assimilation. At an individual level, it brings to mind people who work to gain acceptance by dressing in ways consistent with the norms of the dominant culture, who ensure fluency in language including adoption of locally accepted idioms, who follow mainstream patterns of cultural consumption and perhaps even abbreviate or change their names into ones more common within the host culture. At a state level it evokes policies in some countries, such as France, that discourages displays of cultural distinctiveness and promotes acceptability through conforming to the norms of the host society. In France, this includes not gathering data based on ethnic or racial groups on the grounds that this would be discriminatory and promote separate identities. A consequence is that it is almost impossible to gather data on the social and economic welfare of ethnic groups, despite testimony of widespread discrimination in areas such as employment, education and housing (Hargreaves, 1995).

Berry identifies marginalisation at the other end of the spectrum as occurring 'when there is little possibility or interest in heritage cultural maintenance (often for reasons of enforced cultural loss), and little interest in having relations with others (often for reasons of exclusion or discrimination)' (Berry, 2005 p705). In this sense, marginalisation may be seen as consistent with the experiences of many asylum seekers and refugees. A refugee is formally identified as someone who has left their country of origin owing to a well-founded fear of persecution. This may be for a variety of reasons including belonging to a particular ethnic or religious group, political organisation or persuasion, or having a particular sexual orientation. For refugees, their culture of origin may be seen as dangerous and oppressive, and they may not be enthusiastic to associate with people from their home country or region when they have fled to another country. To borrow terminology offered by exponents of social capital, they may not seek to 'bond' with those from the same ethnic or cultural groups. They may simultaneously be unwilling or unable to develop 'bridging' with those from the host society in contexts where the host society is viewed as being hostile and potentially dangerous.

This can generate complex and challenging problems in relations between refugees and service providers who are trying to support them in countries of arrival. Service providers may think it will be good for refugees to have contact with people from the same countries and religious groups as they are from, so they can experience the benefits of community bonding following the losses involved in leaving countries and communities of origin. The author saw this when evaluating a programme called 'safe case transfer' in which around 30 unaccompanied asylum-seeking boys aged 16–17 were moved from accommodation in South East

England to Greater Manchester. To make the boys 'feel at home', social workers ensured they were placed near mosques and Afghani community centres, and in ethnically diverse areas. They were perplexed when the boys were not always appreciative of these efforts and expressed some bafflement that English social workers wanted them to be close to cultural and ethnic groups similar to ones they had fled from. Instead some said explicitly that they wanted to be with 'normal English families' and were even perturbed by the ethnic diversity in the areas they were sent to (Watters, 2008).

A common orientation towards addressing the wellbeing of refugees is one in which they are viewed principally as suffering a profound sense of loss owing to their forced migration. Service providers routinely try to compensate as far as they can for this loss by facilitating contact with people and communities refugees may be familiar with. This is a perfectly understandable and well-intentioned response. However, it may be ill judged for two reasons. One is that the service provider may have a naïve idea about what a refugee's 'own community' may consist of and assume that, say, contact with a fellow Afghani Muslim will be welcomed because they have the same nationality and are ostensibly from the same religious group. However, it may well be the case that, while there are some commonalities, there are significant differences, for example, arising from political orientation, religious groups within Islam, tribal affiliations and personal values. The fact that the contact may speak the same, or similar, language, and/or be from the same region, may be a source of mistrust rather than trust. They may be viewed as someone with affiliations in the home country that may be potentially harmful to the refugee, or a potential source of malicious gossip about his life in the UK. It may also be ill-judged as a preoccupation with the effects of loss may result in an inadequate level of engagement with migrant and refugees aspirations and dreams.

Thus marginalisation is expressed as distancing from both the person's own cultural group and the host society, and occupies the other end of the spectrum to assimilation. In the case of refugees assimilation may be a desired state but rejection by a host society results in marginalisation. Two intermediate strategies identified by Berry are separation and integration. Separation relates to an orientation towards cultural maintenance and minimising interaction with a dominant cultural group. It suggests high levels of bonding social capital maximising the benefits of trusting relationships within the cultural group while making little effort to connect with wider society. A good example of this may be provided by religious groups such as the Amish and Mennonite Christians in Pennsylvania. There is a strong emphasis and effort to ensure the maintenance of customs and traditions passed from generation to generation and robust measures taken to control cultural influences from outside the community. Contact with the outside society is generally amicable, but minimised to that which is necessary to ensure the economic wellbeing of the community, such as taking goods to markets in neighbouring cities to sell and running restaurants, cafes and shops for visitors. As Berry indicates, these strategies can display significant variability. The Amish may be an extreme example but are illustrative of an orientation towards separation that may be present in less pronounced ways in other communities.

The second intermediate strategy is one that receives particular attention in Berry's model and has been of notable significance in identifying relations between acculturation, wellbeing and mental health. Berry has defined integration in the following terms: 'When there is an interest in both maintaining one's heritage culture while in daily interactions with other groups, integration is the option. In this case, there is some degree of cultural integrity maintained, and at the same time seeking, as a member of an ethnocultural group, to participate as an integral part of the larger social network' (Berry and Sabatier, 2011 p26). The weight of evidence in acculturation studies points to this strategy as having more benefits in terms of wellbeing and mental health. As Berry notes in reviewing the research evidence, 'the integration way of acculturating is usually associated with better psychological adaptation. This was argued to be the case because by engaging in the two cultures, individuals have dual competencies, and dual networks for social support during the challenges of acculturation. This conclusion has been evaluated by a meta-analysis' of findings across numerous studies' (Berry and Sabatier, 2011, p.664).

In one of a number of studies supporting this view, Brown et al. note that 'on a variety of well-being indicators – life satisfaction, self-esteem, social adjustment – people holding 'integrationist' or bicultural attitudes often score higher than those who are oriented toward just one cultural group' (Brown et al., 2013, p.1657). A large-scale longitudinal study conducted by the author and colleagues from a number of UK universities examined acculturation strategies among schoolchildren in Kent and Sussex, and concluded that integration had the best outcomes for wellbeing and educational performance. The authors argued it was not only better for children of South Asian heritage who were the principle subjects of the study, but also for host society children too. One caveat was that children from the minority group who tried to integrate appeared to display more emotional problems, suggesting possibly an element of sadness or frustration that their efforts at contact were not always reciprocated by host society children (ibid, 2013).

Arguably, a good example of a successful integrationist strategy is the approach adopted by Gujarati communities in the UK. Many Gujaratis arrived in the UK having been expelled by nationalist governments in East Africa in the 1970s. In my own fieldwork among Gujaratis in England in the 1980s, I was struck by how upwardly mobile many were, moving from poorer areas in east London to wealthy suburbs in NW London and Surrey. Many excelled in business and made strenuous efforts to ensure their children went to the best possible schools and universities. Gujarati caste association meetings were notable for large and high profile donations to charities as well as the presence of senior politicians from major political parties. Many in the second generation did not follow parents into business but diversified careers into journalism, politics, academia, the arts, law and medicine. School success was significantly higher than the average for white British students (although not as high as for those of Chinese heritage) and average earnings exceeded those of any British ethnic group including white British (Gov.UK 2018). A distinguishing feature of the Gujarati communities was a strong cultural continuity in terms of religious practice, including support and engagement with Hindu temples in the UK and maintenance of customs and traditions in the home, while simultaneously an active and robust engagement with education and careers, culture, politics and the arts within wider British society. This is not to suggest that the Gujarati story is one of uniform success. The 'community' is diverse and includes Muslims as well as Hindus and people from a range of castes and economic backgrounds who may have differing economic prospects and outcomes. However, the overall picture is generally positive and, in the main, accompanied by what may be defined as an integrationist orientation.

The evidence reviewed above points to the importance of social contact and engagement as a vital component in promoting and maintaining mental health and wellbeing. Within environments with significant cultural diversity, the most beneficial form of engagement is one that encompasses both one's own ethnic or cultural group and wider communities within the host society. In terms of social capital this requires both bonding and bridging social capital, while in terms of acculturation strategies, it requires the adoption of an integrationist orientation. However, the development of bridging social capital and integration are not necessarily matters of choice. Racism and discrimination in societies may prevent the possibility of integration and lead minority groups to experience deep frustrations. It is important therefore to distinguish between those individuals and groups who may choose to remain separate and those who experience an enforced separation owing to laws, policies and attitudes within wider society. This separation may be a consequence of migration status, for example, asylum seekers who experience residential segregation and whose access to welfare support is dependent on agreeing only to live within certain proscribed accommodation.

Exercise 2.2 Enhancing Integration

Given the evidence of the mental health and wellbeing benefits of integration both to minority groups and to the host society, consider practical strategies that may be developed by mental health, social care or social welfare services to enhance integration. For example, are there steps that can be taken in terms of the literature offered by the service to promote an orientation towards integration? What may be the challenges faced in implementing a strategy to promote integration?

Sweden provides an interesting example. On the one hand Sweden is well known for opening doors to asylum seekers and refugees from around the world. However, once in the country and even after achieving citizenship, those who arrived initially as asylum seekers and their children have disproportionately high rates of unemployment and residential segregation. As noted in a National Public Health Report: 'Discrimination in the labour market is a significant factor in low incomes and unemployment. Discrimination in the housing market combined with relative poverty leads to increased concentration of the foreign-born population in low-status neighbourhoods and a decline in the percentage of Swedish- born residents in these areas' (Hjern, 2012, p.225). Research has also indicated a pronounced risk of suicide among second generation men of immigrant backgrounds (Dunlavy et al., 2017). It is notable that this occurs in particular in the second generation, suggesting that the frustration of getting a job is more acute than among the generation who first arrived in Sweden. Further problems among second generation migrants has been noted by Hjern: 'With regard to serious psychosocial health problems such as suicide and psychoses children of immigrants run greater risks than immigrants themselves. These problems are at least as widespread – and, in the case of illicit drug abuse, considerably greater – among children who have grown up in Sweden as among their immigrant parents. Frustrations among second generation migrants were expressed through widespread rioting in 2013 and the large scale burning of cars in the summer of 2018 (EU Observer, 15th August 2018). Many immigrants from the first generation arrived speaking little or no Swedish and have had the challenge of adapting to a new culture. For the second generation however, they speak the language, have relatively good school performance and yet often find themselves marginalised and unemployed. This suggests an impulse towards integration that may have been thwarted and the development of a sense of hostility towards the host society. In turn there is growing antagonism towards immigrants as evidenced by the surge in support for a far-right anti-immigrant party in the run up to elections in 2018.

This example highlights the fact that an orientation towards integration or assimilation on the part of immigrants themselves does not necessarily ensure that integration takes place. As Hewstone has argued: 'A society in which Blacks live apart from Whites, Catholics from Protestants, or French Muslims from their non-Muslim counterparts is not going to deliver safety, peace, and justice for all. We have to aspire to something more than that, an integrated community of fellow-citizens' (Hewstone, 2015, p.434). For integration to be realised, there needs to be efforts made to encourage contact between groups thus pointing towards the role of government agencies and civic society. It further raises questions about how groups are represented in advertising, the media, in information leaflets and websites. A further challenge is indicated in academic research where it is argued that contact with members of the dominant group 'seems to reduce disadvantaged group members' interest in measures that would increase social justice and benefit their group' (Tausch et al., 2015). In other words a sense of solidarity that underpins collective action may be eroded through positive contact. However, Tausch et al. also point out that 'contact with members of advantaged groups positively predicts individuals' motivation to achieve upward mobility'. The authors acknowledge that this presents an intriguing area for further research and debate (Tausch, 2015, p.536). An underlying challenge here is the very construction of social groups and the presumed sovereignty of group membership in governing individuals' personal orientations.

As noted, the idea of fixed 'advantaged' and 'disadvantaged' groups determined by race and ethnicity has been challenged by empirical research pointing to dramatically differing trajectories of upward mobility for example between different South Asian and African groups in the UK (e.g. IPPR, 2007). Emerging research evidence points to the importance of developing more nuanced approaches towards researching the mental health and wellbeing of different populations within different national contexts. Moreover, the very construction of groups themselves may be questionable. As Sennett has observed, emotional and cognitive capacities are erratically realised in modern societies and may not be reducible to examining pre-defined groups and the roles of institutions. In praising the development of 'capabilities theory' by Amartya Sen and Martha Nussbaum, he argues that, 'human beings are capable of doing more than schools, workplaces, civil organisations and political regimes allow for ... people's capacities for cooperation are far greater and more complex than institutions allow them to be' (Sennett, 2013, p.29). The question of the constructions of social and cultural groups is returned to below.

Capabilities, wellbeing and mental health

The development of the capabilities approach marks a radical departure from economically based models for assessing wellbeing and the quality of lives. Until the development of the approach, it was routine to answer the question 'how well is a country doing?'

with reference to measures of gross domestic product. Those countries, or states within countries, with the highest Gross Domestic Product (GDP) were presumed to be the most advanced and best places to live. The Nobel Prize winning economist Amartya Sen pointed out that this formulation only, at best, told a partial story and said little about the overall wellbeing of the populations within particular countries and states. In a comparative study of Indian states carried out by Dreze and Sen, they showed that increased economic growth does not automatically improve quality of life in important areas such as health and education (Dreze and Sen, 2002). A further weakness was that it did not reveal how well particular groups in the population were doing. Sen took African American groups in the US as an example. While the US is the leading country in terms of GDP, he demonstrated that African Americans had poorer levels of mortality and morbidity than Indians living in the state of Kerala. A broader weakness was that GDP did not reveal how satisfactory different countries were at providing basic needs for their populations, for example, food, shelter, security, education and healthcare (Sen, 1999).

Sen and the American philosopher Martha Nussbaum developed the capabilities approach as a corrective to the idea that GDP itself could explain how well countries and populations were doing. The approach emphasised both the quality and availability of institutions and social support and the extent to which this matched the needs and aspirations of the population. The central question lying at the core of the approach is 'what is each person able to do and to be?' As Nussbaum notes, 'the approach is *focussed on choice or freedom,* holding that the crucial good societies should be promoting for their people is a set of opportunities, or substantial freedoms, which people may or may not exercise in action: the choice is theirs' (Nussbaum 2011, p.18). Both Sen and Nussbaum stress the importance of combining concern with the facilities and opportunities provided within countries *and* nurturing human agency, so that people can determine their own life courses. Capabilities, according to Nussbaum, 'are not just abilities residing within a person, but also the freedoms or opportunities created by a combination of personal abilities and the political, social and economic environment' (2011, p.20).

According to Sen and Nussbaum a central question in considering the development of capabilities is 'what does a life worthy of human dignity require?' Nussbaum proposes ten 'Central Capabilities' that, she argues, any decent political order must secure at least at a threshold level for 'all citizens' (Nussbaum, 2011 p33). These are as follows:

1. **Life.** Being able to live to the end of a human life of normal length; not dying prematurely, or before one's life is so reduced as to be not worth living.
2. **Bodily health.** Being able to have good health, including reproductive health; to be adequately nourished; to have adequate shelter.
3. **Bodily integrity.** Being able to move freely from place to place; to be secure against violent assault, including sexual assault and domestic violence; having opportunities for sexual satisfaction and for choice in matters of reproduction.
4. **Senses, imagination, and thought.** Being able to use the senses, to imagine, think, and reason—and to do these things in a "truly human" way, a way informed and cultivated by an adequate education, including, but by no means limited to,

literacy and basic mathematical and scientific training. Being able to use imagination and thought in connection with experiencing and producing works and events of one's own choice, religious, literary, musical, and so forth. Being able to use one's mind in ways protected by guarantees of freedom of expression with respect to both political and artistic speech, and freedom of religious exercise. Being able to have pleasurable experiences and to avoid nonbeneficial pain.

5. **Emotions**. Being able to have attachments to things and people outside ourselves; to love those who love and care for us, to grieve at their absence; in general, to love, to grieve, to experience longing, gratitude, and justified anger. Not having one's emotional development blighted by fear and anxiety. (Supporting this capability means supporting forms of human association that can be shown to be crucial in their development.)

6. **Practical reason**. Being able to form a conception of the good and to engage in critical reflection about the planning of one's life. (This entails protection for the liberty of conscience and religious observance.)

7. **Affiliation**. (A) Being able to live with and toward others, to recognize and show concern for other human beings, to engage in various forms of social interaction; to be able to imagine the situation of another. (Protecting this capability means protecting institutions that constitute and nourish such forms of affiliation, and also protecting the freedom of assembly and political speech.) (B) Having the social bases of self-respect and non-humiliation; being able to be treated as a dignified being whose worth is equal to that of others. This entails provisions of non-discrimination on the basis of race, sex, sexual orientation, ethnicity, caste, religion, national origin.

8. **Other species**. Being able to live with concern for and in relation to animals, plants, and the world of nature.

9. **Play**. Being able to laugh, to play, to enjoy recreational activities.

10. **Control over one's environment**. (A) Political. Being able to participate effectively in political choices that govern one's life; having the right of political participation, protections of free speech and association. (B) Material. Being able to hold property (both land and movable goods), and having property rights on an equal basis with others; having the right to seek employment on an equal basis with others; having the freedom from unwarranted search and seizure. In work, being able to work as a human being, exercising practical reason and entering into meaningful relationships of mutual recognition with other workers.

(Nussbaum, 2011, pp.33–34)

As to the nature of capabilities themselves, critics have argued that Nussbaum's list has changed little over time and is largely informed by intuition rather than extensive empirical evidence (Clark, 2013). Jaggar argues for example that 'I have found no place in her extensive writings on capabilities where she questions her own authority to decide what should be included on the list and what excluded from it. She expresses no misgivings about the fact, that in taking control of the list, she assumes the prerogative not only of determining the philosophical import of others' contributions but also of assessing their moral worth, thus deciding whose opinions should be respected and whose should be rejected as mistaken and corrupt' (2006, p.314). Nussbaum's approach suggests a role for participative democracy that is limited to ratifying and implementing the central capabilities and using the latter as an evaluative tool to assess government programmes. Critics have also pointed to the limited role for children beyond being viewed as potential adults rather than rights bearing citizens.

Beyond these concerns it is also notable that Nussbaum refers repeatedly to the dignity of citizens. This gives rise to the question of the position of non-citizens in her scheme. This is a particularly important question in considering the potential role of capabilities in multi-ethnic situations where many migrants may not have achieved citizenship or have been excluded from doing so. The case of refugees, asylum seekers and undocumented migrants comes immediately to mind. As Agamben argues, 'in the system of the nation state, the so-called sacred and inalienable rights of man show themselves to lack every protection and reality at the moment in which they can no longer take the form of rights belonging to citizens of a state' (Agamben, 1998, p.126). Given the power and persuasiveness of the capabilities approach, not only in terms of academic debate but in the formulation of public policy, it is important to clarify the extent to which capabilities are linked to citizenship or more widely to ensuring the wellbeing of human beings, whatever their status.

On a practical level, the nation state has sovereignty over its territory and citizens and a central question is what agency is responsible for ensuring the wellbeing of non-citizens. A key challenge is to influence governments to incorporate humanitarian conventions and guidelines into statutory instruments and to highlight the specific barriers faced by non-citizens in receiving essential humanitarian support. An example of the wide range of research oriented action that may be taken is Aspinall and Watters' investigation into equality and human rights issues affecting asylum seekers and refugees in the UK on behalf of the UK Equalities and Human Rights Commission (Aspinall and Watters, 2010). This report highlighted deficiencies and good practices across a range of services including health, education and social care. In another example, international comparative work on the treatment of separated and undocumented children has also highlighted deficiencies in meeting children's human rights and specific requirements under the Convention on the Rights of the Child (Bhabha and Crock, 2007, Ruiz-Casares et al., 2010).

A further criticism of the capabilities approach is that it is fundamentally a Western idea, and incorporating it around the globe, or in relation to non-Western minorities in Western countries, represents a kind of imperialist endeavour. This is a familiar argument and has also been frequently used against the introduction of Western mental health services around the globe. Nussbaum has been robust in her rejection of this criticism arguing that the capabilities approach was the product of wide-ranging collaboration with people from a range of non-Western backgrounds. Moreover, she points out that the idea that human rights is a Western conception is historically incorrect and, as Amartya Sen has shown, 'the constituent elements of the idea of human rights exist in both Indian and Chinese traditions (Nussbaum, 2011, p.103, Sen, 2005). Moreover, the formulation of the Universal Declaration of Human Rights in 1948 was done 'in such a way as to make it acceptable to people from a wide range of cultural and religious traditions' (ibid.).

The capabilities approach has clear complementarities with formulations of wellbeing and offers a way of linking people's innate capacities to their realisation through the opportunities available to them in a given society. While the formulation of the list proposed by Nussbaum could perhaps have involved more discussion and receptivity to others ideas and values, and offered a more comprehensive approach with respect to children and non-citizens, it would be hard to raise objections to its substantive contents. Moreover, Nussbaum argues that the list has been developed in a way that deliberately seeks to avoid conflict with the diverse views on life that are present in a pluralistic society and is not in conflict with metaphysical, epistemological or psychological doctrines that may be controversial between groups (2011, p.182). She adds that a reading of the list would reveal nothing that would not be endorsed by governments that embrace political liberalism but many aspects of it would be challenging to more authoritarian and patriarchal regimes.

It is interesting to consider the more specific question of the relationship of a capabilities approach to mental health within a global and pluralist context. The approach has been particularly influential in relation to international development and much of the research into capabilities and mental health is focussed on issues of poverty in lower- and middle-income countries (LMICs). Trani and Bakhshi, for example, characterise research in the area of poverty and mental health as focussing on two central questions: whether poverty increases the risk of mental disorders ('the social causation pathway') or whether people with mental disorders are at a greater risk to fall into or remain in a state of poverty ('the social drift pathway') (Trani and Bakhshi, 2017, p.404). They argue that in order to fully understand the social, economic and personal impact of mental disability in LMICs, there is a need to engage wider conceptualisations of poverty beyond those that focus on income thresholds. Their view is that the capability approach allows for analysis of a wide range of issues including those that are economic, social and cultural. By adopting participatory methods the approach offers the opportunity to gain deeper understanding of culturally specific dimensions of poverty and how these impact on heterogeneous populations. It places the idea of ability to achieve valued functionings, what an individual can do or be in a given context, at the centre of analysis. By adopting this approach, the authors offer a wide-ranging examination of the interrelationship between capabilities and mental disability offering insights into the ways through which specific dimensions of poverty, and combinations of these, heighten the risks of mental disorders and, conversely, how mental disorders impact on increasing poverty in the sense of losing opportunities to realise valued functionings.

White and colleagues also recognise the value of a capability approach in enhancing understandings of linkages between dimensions of poverty and mental health but promote a broader perspective on the potential for using a capability approach in the mental health field. Their proposal is 'an attempt to extend the remit of mental health initiatives to include a specific focus on supporting individuals and communities to have the freedom and capability to engage in valued functionings, which will provide important opportunities for enhancing SWB (subjective wellbeing)' (White et al., 2016, p.2). They thus move beyond clinical models oriented towards identifying mental disorders and relieving symptoms, towards a view of mental health as involving both personal and social transformations. The capability approach is seen as providing a bridge between micro and macro levels of mental health as well as being sensitive and receptive to cultural views and understandings.

While drawing primarily on research evidence from low and middle income countries, specifically their own research in Zambia and India, White and colleagues also point to the benefits of adopting a capabilities approach with ethnically and culturally diverse popula-tions in Western countries. They cite for example the work of Rose and Thompson in a poor and diverse part of Sydney in which they sought to develop and implement a community development approach informed by the capabilities approach. Rose and Thompson suggest a focus on three interrelated aspects: promoting individual capabilities, enabling environ-mental infrastructure, and developing soft infrastructure. The first of these was promoted by a range of group activities, advocacy support and practical tools, for example, supporting people with preparing CVs, computer and presentational skills. The second aimed towards improving the local environment so that it facilitated a sense of creative space and well-being, through clean-ups, creating spaces for artistic activity, and improving the natural environment. Finally, the development of 'soft infrastructure' involved helping people to experience a sense of shared values in relation to the physical space around them (Rose and Thompson, 2012). This bridging between individual capabilities and the physical settings people live and work in, is also stressed by Shinn, who points to the importance of examining and enhancing the 'mediating structures' that can help capabilities be realised. She notes that these have been largely ignored by Sen and Nussbaum beyond stressing the importance of education and access to markets (Shinn, 2015). Consistent with the orientation of Rose and Thompson's intervention, she demonstrates how crucial the immediate environment may be in terms of functionings and how fruitful a methodology informed by examining bridges between the individual and the environment may be in assessing mental health community interventions.

Exercise 2.3 Working with Capabilities

Consider how effective a capabilities approach may be as 1) a framework for developing a holistic service to promote the wellbeing of a particular group 2) a tool for evaluating the effectiveness of an intervention aimed at enhancing mental health or wellbeing.

Rethinking the role of cultural groups

The three orientations we have explored – social capital, acculturation and capabilities – are all potentially fruitful ways of examining mental health and wellbeing in diverse cultural settings. Social capital and the acculturation appoach provide frameworks for examining relations between groups and between groups and institutions. The emphasis on bridging social capital has been made as a counter to concerns that communities may turn inwards and atmospheres of mutual suspicion may hamper community cohesion. This orientation has been reflected in policy development, for example in relation to funding of community groups in the UK, who have been expected to demonstrate how they have encouraged the development of bridging social capital. As noted, the development of social capital or integration is not wholly within the power of minorities themselves. People and their communities may be disposed towards integration and developing bridging social capital but may be prevented from realising these aspirations by hostile public environments. These environments can truncate the potential for fluidity in cultural engagement and dialogue. However, the extent to which there may be disharmony and segregation needs to be carefully calibrated and assessed in diverse countries and locations. There is a tendency for generalisation, particularly through taking examples from the US and, without sufficient critical scrutiny and reflexivity, suggesting they are applicable elsewhere. Bourdieu for one has warned of this tendency, giving the example of the application of US ideas of race relations to Brazil (Bourdieu and Wacquant, 1999). Putnam's example of people 'hunkering down' in the face of diversity may be true of the US but is not supported by important evidence from the UK.

A broader question concerns the construction of groups themselves. In the sphere of inter-cultural and interethnic relations, researchers often proceed by superimposing ethnic or racial categories on populations and then undertaking an analysis of the interactions between the predetermined groups. So, for example, in a study of acculturation in schools in the UK, researchers divided students into those who were British South Asian, a collectivity that included Indian, Pakistani, Bangladeshi, Sri Lankan and 'other', and those who were white English (Rutland et al., 2012). Longitudinal data on acculturation attitudes was then collected using pictographic representations of children with brown skin and those with white skin. Those with brown skin were the ingroup and those with white skin the outgroup. Mixing of children with brown and white skin at play was represented as an example of integration and so on. Besides noting the British South Asian group contained populations that were first and second generation, and included people from diverse nationalities, both groups were treated as though they were largely homogeneous. This is curious not least because the ascribed 'ingroup' contained children from a range of national backgrounds that included countries that had been in conflict with each other for decades and, in the case of India and Pakistan, conflict so severe as to lead to a relatively recent serious nuclear stand-off. Moreover, the ascribed 'ingroup' group contained a variety of religious and ethnic heritages many of which has not had a history, including a very recent history, of living together harmoniously; Indian Hindus and Muslims, Buddhists and Tamil Christians from Sri Lanka and so on.

A further factor is that category British South Asian contains within it children from heritage backgrounds with widely differentiating levels of achievement in British society. Those children and adults who are from Indian and Sri Lankan backgrounds are linked with some of the highest measures of school success in the UK, employment in prestigious professions and average pay in excess of the white British average. In contrast, those from Pakistani and Bangladeshi heritages have some of the poorest results in schools and have below average wages (Gov UK, 2019, IPPR, 2007). The white English group is treated as though unproblematically homogeneous despite potential variations in social class (working class white English boys are at present the poorest achievers in schools). The research design begins with the assumption that group identification is consistent with skin colour. Having ascribed children to groups, the research process is generative, producing evidence of accul-turation strategies and drawing conclusions about the extent and implications about the adoption of the various strategies such as acculturation, integration and so on.

The approach, which places people into rather monolithic ethnic or racial blocks echoes the observation referred to above made by Amartya Sen that there is a tendency in the UK towards what he terms 'serial monoculturalism', in which groups dwell in hermitically sealed ethnic units rather than multiculturalism, with an implication of fluidity between groups and identities. Sen raises the following issue as to whether groups 'should be catego-rised in terms of inherited traditions, particularly the inherited religion, of the community in which they happen to be born, taking that unchosen identity to have automatic priority over other affiliations involving politics, profession, class, gender, language, literature, social involvements, and many other connections?' (Sen, 2007, p.150). It is helpful to differentiate here between an empirical level of considerable fluidity in what may be termed street level realities and an epistemological level within research communities in which ethnic and cultural categories may be generated as fixed and immutable. As Bourdieu cautioned with respect to academic research on groups; 'To speak of a social space means that one cannot group just anyone with anyone while ignoring the fundamental differences, particularly economic and cultural ones' (Bourdieu, 1985, p.726).

This examination of a not untypical study, is not undertaken to suggest we should move away from examining differences and interactions between ethnic and cultural groups. I suggest such studies may proceed in circumstances in which societies have fairly rigorous, more or less fixed, forms of segregation, demonstrated for example by marked residential divisions, and clear income and opportunity differentials between people of different ethnic or cultural backgrounds. In other words in contexts in which group membership is rigorously ascribed and enforced in a discriminatory manner through government and there is little mixing between identified groups. Apartheid South Africa would be an obvious case in which racial groups trajectories were fixed to solidify disadvantage by ideologically driven governments. Arguably, less extreme but nevertheless tenable examples are provided in some parts of contemporary America and Europe where there are high levels of residential segregation and unemployment among specific ethnic and cultural communities. The broad point here is that there are circumstances in which society, through power relations, consists of discernible, distinctive and durable groups and it is reasonable to conduct studies that explore their interrelations. However, in societies in which there is evidence of high levels of fluidity in respect of upward social mobility, education and employment and considerable ethnic mixing (one in ten couples in the UK for example are ethnically mixed) it may not be reasonable to assume that skin colour will have a determining effect on school performance, occupation, income or residence, and a more nuanced methodological approaches may be suggested.

Exercise 2.4

Consider the example of a mental health or social welfare service that has been established in a location with high ethnic diversity. How would decisions be made with respect to the identities of the populations to be served in the location? What impact are these decisions likely to have on the types of services provided? How would you ensure that people would be able to define their own cultural identities and the services that would be most helpful to them?

One methodological approach allows for a preliminary period of qualitative research in which, to extend the example of children in a mixed school setting, children discuss the groups that are meaningful to them and ethnographic research is conducted to examine how children interact and form groups. Thus the composition of groups is not superimposed by the researchers from their ideas of what constitutes meaningful categories, but is explored 'from the ground up' by children themselves and places their valued relations at the centre of the research. Bourdieu again is instructive here in emphasising the importance of not simply reinforcing and embedding bias present in the social world into categories used in social research. The researcher should instead engage with the views of research participants themselves: 'The most resolutely objectivist theory has to integrate the agents' representation of the social world; more precisely, it must take account of the contribution that agents make towards constructing the view of the social world, and through this, towards constructing this world' (Bourdieu, 1985, p.727).

Rather than approaching studies of group interaction in contexts of cultural diversity by presupposing how groups are constructed, it is helpful to consider firstly what constitutes meaningful groups in the study setting. The proposal is that studies should begin by a preliminary qualitative engagement that is aimed at exploring in depth the categories that are important to participants. An open and engaged approach towards eliciting the views and perspectives of participants will help address the problem Bourdieu highlights of 'reinforcing and embedding bias present in the social world'. The approach also has the merit of demonstrating from the outset that the perspectives of the research subjects are of importance and indeed will offer a guiding framework for the study.

An example is the framework for a study of peer interactions in schools in which there are children from diverse cultural backgrounds. The following, adapted from a proposed study by the author on refugee and migrant children's wellbeing in schools may offer a helpful guide to this approach.

Case Study: Migrant and Refugee Children's Wellbeing in Schools

A helpful orientation towards examining intergroup interactions in this context is to focus on the generation of social capital, specifically the ways in which both bonding and bridging social capital is developed in schools. Previous research has demonstrated the close relationship between bridging social capital and an integrationist approach. This planned intervention provides an opportunity to examine strategies aimed at developing positive peer interactions and social support in the context of multi-ethnic schools. Epistemologically, it recognises the importance of the child's own perspectives on salient groups and networks, rather than presupposing that the imposition of a simple binary will be reflective of the child's own viewpoint. It will be based initially in a school that has introduced refugee children in recent years and has been active in trying to support an integrative approach. The school will offer specific initiatives aimed towards enhancing students integration including classes aimed at appreciating cultural differences.

The intervention aims to enhance the role of schools in promoting cross-group understanding and friendships. It will focus on schools with high diversity but offer an emic approach towards the understanding of groups, rather than presuppose that groups are configured by simple binaries. Initially it will focus on engagement with students themselves in understanding groups in the classroom. Secondly it will offer a creative space for activities exploring issues of understanding and friendship through stories, art and play. Thirdly it will adopt a formative approach to evaluation engaging students, parents and teachers in assessing the drivers and impediments to enhancing understanding and friendships. Fourthly, the intervention aims to understand and implement the drivers of sustainable change. The intervention will be spread over one term (semester) of approximately ten weeks. There will be two 60-minute sessions on the theme of 'exploring networks and groups', six weekly sessions of 60 minutes (this period of time may be changed in consultation with the participating schools timetable) on enhancing contact and friendship.

The sessions will be spread across one school term (semester) and involve an estimated ten sessions. Two preliminary sessions aimed towards developing an emic understanding of groups and networks in the school. It is proposed that one focuses on reception year students (aged 11 and 12) and another aimed at intermediate year. The sessions will be participative and engaged. There is potential for adopting a Q methodology to examine student's own networks and friendships. The results from these sessions will help frame the content of the interventions. There will then be six sessions facilitated by an experienced therapist to work with students in exploring peer relations and what may be done to enhance them. This will include explorations using children's literature and more broadly working with examples of friendships between in-group and out-group members. Students will work with art and play to explore concepts of 'bridges' and 'boundaries' between groups. Two sessions will be held at the end of the term and focus on formative evaluation, drawing together stakeholders to reflect on the shared learning from the intervention and the potential for wider school dissemination and incorporation.

3 | Mental Health and Wellbeing: Perspectives on Religion and Spirituality

Chapter Overview

- Distinctions between religion and spirituality are drawn, highlighting social and personal aspects, and implications for mental health and wellbeing. This includes reflection on 'extrinsic' and 'intrinsic' religiosity.

- Two distinctive religious traditions are examined, Christianity and Buddhism, one oriented principally towards belief in God and prayer, while the other is oriented towards understanding and transcending human suffering. We consider the implications of each for understanding what constitutes mental health and wellbeing.

- The role of prayer in healing is examined and how processes of prayer may be understood as consistent with some therapeutic practices of psychotherapists. Evidence of the beneficial impact of prayer on mental health is considered.

- The role of explanatory models (EMs) is examined and the way in which these may be mediated through patients' social position and cultural contexts. This includes examining 'healing journeys' people may take, in which they may engage with widely differing forms of therapeutic intervention.

It may be helpful at the outset of this chapter to consider two levels at which the relationships between religion and spirituality on the one hand, and wellbeing and mental health on the other, may be explored. The terminology introduced by the psychologist Gordon Allport and colleagues is useful in this context. Allport and his colleague J. Michael Ross distinguish between what they term 'extrinsic' and 'intrinsic' religiosity. They define the extrinsically religious as follows:

> *people of this orientation are disposed to use religion for their own ends ... Extrinsic values are always instrumental and utilitarian. Persons with this orientation may find religion useful in a variety of ways – to provide security and solace, sociability and distraction, status and self-justification. The embraced creed is lightly held or else selectively shaped to fit more primary needs. In theological terms the extrinsic type turns to God, but without turning away from self.*

By contrast, they define the category of 'intrinsically' religious people as: 'Persons [who] find their master motive in religion. Other needs, strong as they may be, are regarded as of less ultimate significance, and they are, so far as possible, brought into harmony with the religious beliefs and prescriptions. Having embraced a creed the individual endeavours to internalize it and follow it fully. It is in this sense that he lives his religion' (Allport and Ross, 1967, p.434).

Allport's motivation was to study prejudice in the two religious groups and, perhaps unsurprisingly, he found higher levels of prejudice among extrinsically religious people, who went to church as a means to develop social relations and status. I use the distinction in a broader manner here, albeit while retaining the distinction between socially and personally oriented religious observance. Extrinsic religiosity relates here to the social and communal aspects of religion – participation in churches, mosques, synagogues, gurdwaras and so on – while intrinsic religiosity relates to the personal level at which religion is experienced – for example through prayer, meditation and contemplation. This distinction is drawn because it helps to clarify some of the mental health and wellbeing issues that may arise from participation in religion. I begin by considering the more social dimensions of religion, before exploring the implications of personal religiosity for mental health and wellbeing. I then consider the extent to which the personal and social dimensions may be interlinked, and the implications of this interlinkage for mental health and wellbeing.

Before proceeding, it is also helpful to consider the relationship between religion and spirituality. These two words are often used interchangeably as though they were synonymous, or the spiritual is seen simply as an integral element of religious practice. In Christianity, for example, the central ritual of the Eucharist is viewed as offering 'spiritual transformation', as bread and wine is transformed by the Holy Spirit into the body and blood of Jesus Christ (Williams, 2014, p.57). However, in contemporary usage spirituality is often seen as something distinct from religion. Research has indicated that approximately one fifth of people in Britain and one quarter of the US population regard themselves as 'spiritual, but not religious' (King et al., 2013; BBC, 2013). A common idea is that spirituality may be present outside of organised religion, indeed, many people who describe themselves as spiritual do so to differentiate themselves from adherents of formal religions. According to a report by the BBC, '"spiritual, but not religious" represents a major strand of belief across the West. The spiritually aligned range from pagans to devotees of healing crystals, among many other sub-groups. But for millions of others it is nothing so esoteric. Instead, it's simply a "feeling" that there must be something else' (BBC, 2013).

One perspective is offered by the neuroscientist Sam Harris, who locates spirituality within the specific realm of experiences that bring a deep sense of a transcendent reality, as 'when you have certain experiences in meditation, or with psychedelics, that show you a very different possibility for your experiences, moment to moment'. He argues however, that these spiritual experiences are distinct from theorising about the nature of reality, 'those don't tell you anything about the nature of the cosmos. You can't extrapolate from a feeling of unconditional love, for instance, to a belief that the energy of love pervades the cosmos, that it preceded the Big Bang or anything like that, which is a very common New Age-kind of extrapolation' (2015). The sharp distinction between an experiential level and theoretical one is challenged however by interrelationships between experiences garnered for example through meditation and the development of frameworks for understanding mind and body as found in Buddhism, Jainism and some Hindu traditions. Moreover, this kind of extrapolation is common among people who regard themselves as 'spiritual, but not religious'.

Ammerman argues that the commonly held view that religion is in decline and is being replaced by an individualised spirituality is too simplistic, and that spirituality itself is a complex phenomenon with people constructing meanings of spirituality that may incorporate aspects of, and affinities to, organised religion (2013). She outlines a range of different types of spirituality, including one rooted in belief in a single god or gods, and another based on a sense of transcendence, often experienced through links to the natural world – akin to what may have once been referred to in the West as romanticism. The variety of views on the relationship between religion and spirituality indicate that it may be helpful to consider a spectrum of perspectives. On one level this may range from a socially to a spiritually oriented religiosity (akin to the concept of extrinsic religiosity proposed by Allport and Ross), and on another from a spirituality that resides within a tradition of organised religion (consistent with the idea of spiritual transformation offered by Williams, below) and a spirituality that dispenses with forms of organised religion.

This may be represented as follows:

Socially-oriented religiosity (extrinsic)		Spiritually-oriented religiosity (intrinsic)
Spirituality with links to organised religion and views informed by religious tradition	⬅➡	Spirituality outside of organised religion

Wellbeing and the social dimensions of religion

In considering the social dimension of religion, there is evidence linking religious involvement with enhanced social capital. De Tocqueville, in his seminal study *Democracy in America* (2003), argued that democracy requires the presence and vitality of civic associations that are not necessarily political in nature but serve as sources of meaning and social engagement. Putnam has followed de Tocqueville in placing the presence of associational life at the heart of his concept of social capital. As we have noted, social capital, in the forms of trust and participation, has in turn been associated with protection against mental health problems (Davidson et al., 2016). As Haslam and colleagues have noted: 'Evidence suggests that the more sources of social support we have the better the effect on our health' (Haslam et al., 2009, p.329).

Engagement with religious organisations can be a major source of associative life for millions of people around the globe, offering potentially high levels of participation and networks of trust. As Luhrmann notes, there is significant evidence for the positive impact of church attendance: 'Scholars have known for some time that weekly church attendance keeps people healthy ... One study reports that on average, in the United States, it adds 2 or 3 years to one's life. Another found a 7-year difference in life expectancy at age 20 between those who never attended church and those who attended more than once a week. Religious observance boosts the immune system and decreases blood pressure' (Luhrmann, 2013, p.707). Participation is generated from the wide range of activities that religious organisations initiate and conduct. Beyond the core of formal participative religious services – weekly Mass at church, formal weekly prayer at a mosque, weekly devotional rites at a Hindu temple and so on – religions are often involved in associated charitable, educational and cultural activities. A glance at a parish bulletin board from a small provincial English city reveals the following activities: prayer groups (some directed at specific issues of social concern, such as euthanasia, while others are directed towards silent undirected contemplation), national and international pilgrimages, bereavement workshops, charity walks and bike rides, meetings to plan social events, music and scripture groups. Alongside weekly meetings, there are ongoing charitable activities, for example, in support of overseas missionaries, helping the homeless and poor in the parish and support for migrants and refugees in northern France. Religious services and parish activities cover the entire lifespan, from baptismal rituals to services for the sick and funerals. A Buddhist monastery in the south-east of England identifies in its newsletter a wide range of activities: from participation in retreats to joining a women's network and joining in a family summer camp. Lay people can participate in weekly talks and daily pujas, and members of the monastic community accept invitations to visit the sick and conduct funerals (Forest Sangha Newsletter Summer, 2018). A similarly wide range of activities are organised by local mosques, Hindu temples and Sikh gurdwaras. The lists suggest a wide variety of ways in which associative life may be enhanced through involvement with organised religions. A shared religious affinity also suggests that there is likely to be a common base of values and beliefs, making it easier to form the networks of trust that are central to social capital.

The link between religious participation and social capital can be theorised at both macro and micro levels. At a macro level, social capital has been conceptualised as the features of social organisations that facilitate coordination and cooperation for the benefit of all members of the organisation (Yeary et al., 2012). In this context, the various groups, clubs and shared charitable activities that are generated by religious organisations constitute macro level social capital, while the micro level includes the more individualised forms of association and networks of trust that are formed by participants. It is important to add that these activities and networks have both local and international dimensions. They concern face-to-face relations in the immediate environment as well as linkages to people and places around the world, where other followers of the religion may be based. These dimensions interpenetrate, as religious personnel such as priests, nuns, imams and monks are part of a global religious community and are likely to have had experiences in various international contexts. A common (or only slightly variant) form of religious service (including devotional chants, liturgies, rituals and ceremonies) thus may link participants to transnational communities in the Indian sub-continent, Europe, the Americas and so on.

The transnationalism of major organised religions is of particular significance with respect to the social capital of migrant communities. Those arriving in a new country can have points of reference to beliefs and practices reflecting familiar life in their home countries. They may also have the opportunity to connect and interact with networks of people from their own countries, speaking the same language and sharing values that they are familiar with. For example, the English parish referred to above hosts a Polish community mass and association, as well as services for the Syro-Malabar Catholic community (composed of migrants from the Indian state of Kerala). The aforementioned Buddhist monastery serves significant numbers of people from the Thai and Sri Lankan communities living in the UK, as well as Western practitioners.

In the US context, it has been noted that churches have often filled a gap generated by a decline in other forms of civic association, such as unions and cultural associations. Because they occupy a social space that is neither governed by markets nor by the state, these may be particularly generative spaces, and have given rise to numerous charities, civil rights movements and arts and cultural endeavours (Smidt, 2003). Religious leaders often play influential political roles, as they can wield significant influence on the populations that they serve, and thus act as bridges between the people and the state. This role is less marked in Western Europe, however, where Christianity, while not without significant influence with its adherents, has a diminishing influence on civic society.

There are significant opportunities for participation and networking in the 'associative spaces' generated by organised religions. However, in light of the observations of Allport and Ross regarding increased prejudice among church-going 'extrinsically' religious populations, it should also be noted that while religious participation can enhance social wellbeing, it may be marginalising for those with mental health problems. There are certainly instances in which people with mental health problems have been excluded from religious congregations and communities, and experience shame and guilt but it would be inappropriate to generalise from some specific examples (Davidson et al., 2016). There are of course a wide disparity in religious organisations and in mental health conditions. Furthermore, as Allport and Ross note, distinct groups exist within congregations, with a wide range of motivations and value systems that inform how they relate to their religion. There is some evidence to suggest that people who report religious belief and practice experience better mental and physical health than those who do not (Koenig and Larson, 2001; Wong et al., 2006). It is however difficult to discern which aspects of religious belief or practice are most conducive to good mental health, and whether the potential benefits may be outweighed by aspects of belief or practice that may be detrimental. What's more, there may be differences in social support offered by religious organisations in different countries. King et al. has noted that, 'given that religious participation in English society is a minority activity, it may be that the social support intrinsic to a more religious society is missing' (2013, p.72), concluding that non-religious people who hold spiritual beliefs have less emotional stability and are more prone to mental health problems.

The difficulties in evaluating the impact of religion and spirituality are highlighted by Koenig who argues, 'While religious beliefs and practices can represent powerful sources of comfort, hope, and meaning, they are often intricately entangled with neurotic and psychotic disorders, sometimes making it difficult to determine whether they are a resource or a liability' (Koenig, 2009, p.283). He argues that, 'systematic research published in the mental health literature to date does not support the argument that religious involvement usually has adverse effects on mental health', and moreover it may be related to, 'better coping with stress and less depression, suicide, anxiety, and substance abuse' (ibid., p.289). Recent anthropological research is supportive of Koenig's findings. In her exploration of the culture and the experience of mental illness, Janis Jenkins writes, 'my data offer no grounds to suggest that religious experience is symptomatic of psychopathology or that religious activity can cause or exacerbate mental illness' (Jenkins, 2015, p.211).

Exercise 3.1 Considering Religion and Wellbeing

Consider examples in which religion may be a source of comfort, hope and meaning to someone experiencing mental distress. How are the qualities of comfort, hope and meaning likely to be manifested? Are there examples you can think of in which religious belief or practice may exacerbate mental distress?

While there has been significant academic debate on the relationship between religion and mental health, a much broader issue is the extent to which wellbeing may be affected by religious beliefs and practices. A fundamental question here is how ideas of wellbeing are constituted within major religious traditions. When considering the importance of this, it is worth bearing in mind the proportion of the world's population that may still be regarded as 'religious'. Even in circumstances in which people may not be regular attendees of religious services, or regular practitioners of religious rites, it is reasonable to assume that the dominant religious tradition in their countries of origin continues to have a significant impact on how they reflect on what constitutes human wellbeing.

While it is beyond the scope of this book to comment on all religious traditions, it is illustrative to reflect briefly on what two major religious traditions – Christianity and

Christians are the largest religious group in 2015

% of world population

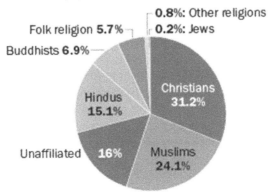

Number of people in 2015, in billions

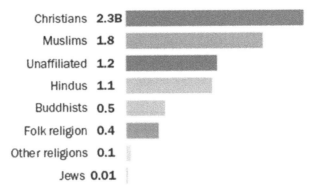

Figure 3.1 World Religions as % of World Population
Source: Pew Research Center demographic projections.
See Methodology for details.
"The Changing Global Religious Landscape"
PEW RESEARCH CENTER

Buddhism – can tell us about what constitutes human wellbeing, and on the impact of these ideas in contemporary societies. Christianity, according to the Pew Research Center, has the largest number of adherents around the world, and is the largest religion in the West. Buddhism is estimated to be followed by 6.9% of the world population. Its influence however far exceeds the number of adherents and can be observed in the worldwide spread of its meditation techniques – most notably 'mindfulness' (*sati*) – that have been embraced by millions of secular practitioners. In the second half of the book we will go on to consider the role of cultural and religious ideas and practices in shaping interventions and models for the enhancement of wellbeing.

Christian religious practice and wellbeing

The former Archbishop of Canterbury and leading theologian Rowan Williams has identified the essence of Christianity as consisting of four components: baptism, Bible, Eucharist and prayer (Williams, 2014). The emphasis placed on each of these elements varies across Christian churches. The Eucharist is more central to Catholic, Anglican and Orthodox traditions, while Bible reading is arguably more associated with Protestant traditions. Baptism and prayer are core aspects of every Christian tradition. For Christians, suffering and redemption underpin each of the elements identified by Williams. Baptism – the original meaning of which is literally 'dipping' – is a form of spiritual rebirth through being immersed in water. Through baptism, one participates in the story of the creation, in which God created the world out of primordial waters. Williams argues that, 'baptism means being with Jesus "in the depths": the depths of human need, including the depths of our own selves in their need – but also the depths of God's love; in the depths where the Spirit is re-creating and refreshing human life as God meant it to be' (2014, p.4). Most fundamentally, baptism is an initiation into the Christian faith, the point at which one becomes a Christian, a follower of the teaching of Jesus Christ. At this point the person is seen as entering into a fundamental connection with God and a global community with other Christians, but also with what Williams refers to as the 'suffering and muddle of the human world'. Indeed, the idea of community is fundamental to Christians. The community of baptised Christians is, 'a great economy of giving and exchange' made possible through the gifts of prayer and love. Redemption in this context is not only sought though an effort to develop personal holiness, but also via an engagement with, and support for, others. According to Pope Francis, sanctification is achieved from a personal mission that is inseparable from the building a kingdom of 'love, justice and universal peace on earth' (2018, p.15). He cautions people against isolation in their religious lives, arguing that, 'it is not healthy to love silence while fleeing interaction with others, to want peace and quiet while avoiding activity, to seek prayer while disdaining service' (ibid.).

There are, of course, different traditions within Christianity, including contemplative orders that live in relative isolation from the outside world. However, these are rare, and for the vast majority of Christians a commitment to 'good works' involves service to the community, particularly the poor, as a defining part of holy life. Prayer can be a solitary or a communal activity, but in the major Christian traditions (I exclude here some evangelical churches that integrate aspiration for personal wealth into prayer), it is not intended to be oriented towards personal or communal gain, and is inseparable from striving towards a realisation of the kingdom of God on Earth. According to Williams', prayer begins with a vision of the world that is transparent to God: 'May your kingdom come your will be done, may what you (God) want shine through in this world and shape the kind of world it is going to be' (2014, p.63).

From the perspective of models of wellbeing, one can identify synergies with several of the components that we have identified. For example, the 'Five Ways to Wellbeing', proposed by the New Economics Foundation, are as follows: 'connect, be active, take notice, learn, and give' (New Economics Foundation, 2018). The altruistic and communitarian orientation of Christian practice suggests enhanced engagement with the first and the last of these aspects. There is considerable emphasis on connecting with others in love and prayer, and churches can be fruitful locations for social engagement. While Christian practice is not specifically oriented towards leading a physically and/or mentally active life (in the sense of incorporating exercise regimes such as yoga and meditation), engagement does, at the very least, provide encouragement to attend services and participate more fully in the community. Edward Fischer's (2014) formulation of wellbeing, discussed earlier, includes the element of 'commitment to a larger purpose', which is strongly correlated with religious practices, including Christianity. We will return to this aspect below.

Buddhism, mental health and wellbeing

While major world religions such as Christianity, Islam and Judaism are centred on belief in, and worship of, God, the core of Buddhist practice is centred on what may be described as a phenomenological investigation of the human condition. The Buddha was a man who was born in the 6th Century BC, in what is now the border region between India and Nepal, and spent his life in what are now the Indian states of Bihar and Uttar Pradesh. The story of the Buddha is that of a prince who grew up amidst all of the luxuries that life could offer. His palace was a place of sensual delights, and legend has it that his father kept him there so that he would be shielded from the sufferings and deprivations of life. It was felt that, if he did observe these things, he would be inclined to abandon his princely life and become a religious seeker. However, at one point he stole away from the palace and saw a succession of people who revealed the realities of human suffering, including an old man, a sick man and a dying man. The fourth person he saw was a wandering *sadhu*, or holy man, and he was impressed by the serenity of his countenance and decided to leave the palace and his worldly goods in a quest for liberation from human suffering. The Buddha initially followed the ascetic practices of the times, which involved fasting and subjecting the body and mind to extreme austerities, before abandoning these in favour of what came to be known as the Buddhist 'Middle Way' between sensory indulgence and extreme asceticism. After gaining enlightenment, he spent the next 40 years of his life wandering in present day India, founding a monastic order (the '*bhikkhu sangha*') and teaching to monks and lay people.

Buddhism is oriented around four 'noble truths', the first of which is the truth of human suffering. Buddhists are encouraged to reflect on the ubiquity of suffering in the human condition: that birth, old age, sickness and death are suffering (for instance, not getting what you want is suffering, just as getting what you don't want is also suffering). The second noble truth is of the origin of this suffering, which is seen as rooted in human craving or desire – the desire for things to be other than they are. The third noble truth is the end of suffering, in which relentless desire is extinguished when a person reaches a state of *nirvana* or *nibbana* (depending on whether adherents follow the Sanskrit or Pali traditions of Buddhism). Having identified suffering, its cause and its end, Buddhist teaching then identifies the 'noble eightfold path' which adherents should follow to end suffering. This consists of right understanding, right intention, right speech, right action, right livelihood, right effort, right mindfulness and right concentration. It is sufficient here to note that the path is oriented around three aspects – ethics, meditation and wisdom. In many traditional Buddhist countries, lay people's practice is focussed on developing ethical standards of conduct, while meditation leading to insight and wisdom is the province of Buddhist monks. The core of Buddhist ethics rests in five precepts – to not kill, to not steal, to refrain from sexual misconduct, not to tell lies and to refrain from intoxicating drink and drugs. In the West however, people are most often drawn to Buddhism by the practice of meditation, and the development of ethics generally follows some experience in meditation practices.

At the most fundamental level, meditation is about bringing attention to the present moment and typically commences by noting moods and physical sensations. Meditation may be explained as consisting of two types of practice. The first, *samatha*, refers to the concentration of the mind on an object. A common object used is the breath or a mantra, and focussing on either is seen as having a calming effect on the mind. The practice of *samatha* can generate a feeling of calm, and regular application of the practice can result in states of deep absorption and tranquillity. Samatha, particularly in the form of concentration on the breath, is often seen as a necessary preliminary to the development of insight. In itself, it is seen as a very pleasant and beneficial practice and has been a component of a number of religious traditions in a variety of forms, for example, Sufism in Islam, meditation traditions in Hinduism and the 'Jesus prayer' in Christianity.

The second, and most distinctive Buddhist form of meditation is *vipassana*, or insight meditation. This involves being fully aware of the present moment, the movement of the breath, the sensations in the body, thoughts and emotions. Vipassana may be seen as an intensive form of mindfulness practice, or *sati*, which refers to ongoing awareness of body, mind and emotions in all of the human postures (sitting, standing, walking or lying down). The goal of Buddhist practice is to develop mindfulness to the point at which there is ongoing seamless awareness. In practicing awareness, the adherent learns a form of 'radical acceptance', whereby all of the conditions of mind and body are noted and, without attachment, are let go of (Brach, 2004). According to meditation instructors, a consequence of this practice is that the mind becomes still and calm, regardless of the level of external or internal disturbance, whether on a silent meditation retreat or riding the London Underground. The still mind can be a vehicle for deepening one's insight into the nature of human existence and the causes of suffering. Existence can be seen as having three characteristics or 'marks' – 'impermanence' (*anicca*), 'suffering' (*dukkha*) and 'no-self' (*anatta*). In the Buddhist traditions the correct orientation is not that of 'belief' in these teachings, but rather of viewing them as items for phenomenological investigation.

On the face of it, Christianity and Buddhism present very different perspectives on wellbeing and mental health. The emphasis in Christianity is on a creator God, a father who sent his son to earth to save people from sin and teach a gospel of love and redemption. The Christian practice is one of professing belief in God, partaking of sacraments that are witness to God's transformational power, being present to God in prayer, and enacting God's will through service within the community. Buddhism is not oriented towards belief in a god or gods but towards achieving realisation through practice. The path to *nirvana* is not one in which divine intervention is sought but one in which the practitioner is exhorted to 'be a lamp unto yourself'. Socially too there are considerable differences between the two religions. The priest, for example, in the Roman Catholic tradition serves a parish through conducting essential rites of passage, such as births, marriages and funerals. Priests work in the community to spread the Christian gospel, visit the sick and make themselves available as a guide and support for members of the parish community. Buddhist monks (or *bhikkhus*) by contrast do not have – and indeed are explicitly forbidden from having – a role in proselytising. Their rules require them provide services to the community when they have been formally requested to do so. Their role is not to support the poor by providing material and emotional support and there is little equivalent in the Buddhist world to the scale of international charitable missions of Christian churches. Rather it is the job of lay people to support the monks by providing food, shelter and medicines through cultivating the virtue of generosity. In return it is believed lay people will gain merit that will help their wellbeing in this and in future lives. Traditionally Buddhist monks are not allowed to have money and are entitled to only very basic minimal requirements such as food, clothing and medicines.

Despite these differences, there are subtle areas of complementarity and convergence. The *bhikkhu* – particularly one accomplished in meditation – is a resource for the Buddhist lay community and acts as a transmitter of the Buddhist teachings. In doing so he may place them within the context of the culture and 'life world' of the community. The revered Thai meditation teacher Ajahn Chah was celebrated not least for the skill with which he placed Buddhist teaching within the idioms familiar to the poor farming communities in north-eastern Thailand where his monastery was based. Within the Christian context, the priest plays a complementary role of interpreting the gospel through the idioms of everyday language and experiences that his parishioners would understand and would be able to relate to their own lives. Thus both *bhikkhus* and priests act as religious specialists who can offer a gateway towards appreciating the significance of religious teachings for ordinary lives. While the act of giving to the *bhikkhus* is different in form to the support offered to priests by the Christian laity (and the latter are paid a wage by the church), the support for both brings communities together in acts of collective generosity.

Religion and healing

A further aspect of many religious practices is the role of healing. Beliefs in healing through the intervention of deities or spirits are widespread in different cultures around the world. In the Christian context, numerous episodes in the Bible recount Jesus' curing of the blind and the disabled, and even raising the dead. There are also accounts of the healing of those suffering from what might be termed 'spiritual afflictions', such as demonic possession. Given the ubiquity and centrality of these stories in the Gospels, it is perhaps surprising that faith, or spiritual healing, doesn't play a more central role in the services and activities of major Christian churches. In the Catholic tradition, the cessationist school of thought professes that the ability to heal – along with the capacity for prophecy and speaking in tongues – died out in the apostolic age. This perspective is contested by growing charismatic and Pentecostal movements, which argue that these gifts remain available to priests and lay members of congregations.

Whether or not healing forms part of church services or parish activities, Christians themselves may routinely use the language and symbolism of religion in developing 'explanatory models' (EMs) of afflictions of various kinds, and use religiously inspired ceremonies in seeking cures (Taussig, 1982). The anthropologist Thomas Csordas has undertaken extensive studies into healing in the Catholic Pentecostal tradition, which has grown in influence and numbers since the 1960s. He notes three main modalities of Pentecostal healing – physical healing of bodily distress, inner healing of emotional illness and distress and deliverance from the adverse effects of demons or evil spirits (Csordas, 2002, p.14). Physical healing is normally performed simply by the laying on of hands, accompanied by prayer that the sickness be healed, while the other two modalities are 'etiological', in that they are initiated when the cause of the problem is discerned to be spiritual, psychological or demonic. Csordas notes that, despite the very specific and ritualised modalities of Pentecostal healing, there is fluidity and also acceptance of more orthodox and mainstream therapeutic approaches. He notes that: 'Catholic Pentecostals do not reject Western medicine out of hand and are willing to make referrals to conventional practitioners when it is deemed necessary' (ibid., p.16). Practitioners may have training in Western forms of therapy, such as counselling and psychotherapy, and integrate these practices with ritual healing. Csordas notes examples of this integration in practice: 'The Catholic Pentecostal healer by means of gifts of revelation guides the suffering individual through an underworld – not the mythical underworld of shamanism, but the post-Freudian underworld of suppressed memories remythologized by being subjected to religious techniques' (ibid., 2002, p.20). To use terminology introduced by the psychiatrist and anthropologist Arthur Kleinman (1988), and now widely employed in mental health, the patient (the 'supplicant' in the terminology of Christian religious healing) may learn to see her condition in terms of a new explanatory model or EM, that takes it from the domain of medical science or psychotherapy and places it within her religious belief system.

While there is significant emphasis on the benefits that can emerge from religious participation in terms of social capital, there is a need to also consider the implications of religious practice for the inner life. William James, in his classic book *The Varieties of Religious Experience*, characterises prayer in a narrow, 'petitional', sense, and gives the examples of prayer for the sick and for desired weather conditions. He approves of petitional prayer in the first sense, remarking that, 'if any medical fact can be said to stand firm, it is that in certain environments prayer may contribute to recovery' (James, 1985, p.463). However, he is more sceptical on the merits of praying for better weather. Prayer in its wider sense is defined as, 'every kind of inward communion or conversation with the power recognized as divine', and he adds that in this sense every scientific criticism leaves it untouched. He goes on to quote the French theologian Auguste Sabatier who describes prayer as, 'no vain exercise of words, no mere repetition of certain sacred formulae, but the very movement itself of the soul, putting itself in a personal relation of contact with the mysterious power of which it feels the presence' (ibid., p.464). James sees Sabatier's reflections as pointing to the very essence of what religion is: 'The consciousness which individuals have of an intercourse between themselves and higher powers with which they feel themselves to be related' (ibid., p.465).

The anthropologist Tanya Luhrmann has developed a global reputation for her work exploring the interaction between religious practices, the supernatural and mental health. This has included examining different modalities of prayer, and the linkages between prayer and healing. She argues that the health benefits of church attendance – evidenced by greater life expectancy and improvement to the immune system – are not necessarily due to a reduction in physical and mental disorders arising from loneliness and isolation. While not disputing the potentially positive impact of church attendance, Luhrmann believes there may be actual healing taking place, deriving from the process of prayer. She challenges the view of many in the mental health field who see religiosity as having a negative influence on mental health, owing to associations with guilt, denial and failure to grasp reality.

Luhrmann identifies two types of prayer – 'apophatic' and 'kataphatic'. While the first refers to techniques to detach from thought, kataphatic prayer, 'asks people to dwell lovingly on what is imagined, and its techniques help to intensify the imagination in the act' (Luhrmann, 2013, p.712). Together, apophatic and kataphatic prayer, 'engage the senses … evoke vivid memories, and … generate powerful emotions' (ibid.).

Luhrmann found this type of prayer was central to religious practice in American evangelical traditions. It can be added that it is also present in the Ignatian Christian tradition, as founded by St. Ignatius of Loyola and practiced around the globe in the form of the Examen Prayer. This prayer has five steps. Adherents initially open themselves to a 'transition', in which they reflect on God's love in their lives. The next stage involves expressing gratitude for the gift of God's love during the day, followed by a stage called 'petition', asking for wisdom and strength to make the prayer a work of grace beyond human capacity alone. The central part of the prayer is a review of the day to discern what has been the work of God and what has not been the work of God, and the choices and responses that have been made. There is then a request for a healing touch from God, to remove the heart's burdens, and then thinking ahead to the following day and how to live in accordance with God's wishes. The prayer concludes with a further transition, in which God's presence is felt within the person praying (Gallagher, 2006). In contemporary practice, the prayer may be accompanied by a preliminary period of mindfulness practice, focussing on the body and breath. It may also be accompanied by a close reading of a passage of scripture followed by visualisation of what happened in the reading, as though the person praying was a participant in biblical events.

According to Luhrmann's research, the formal structure of these prayer practices has four features: expectancy, epistemic ambiguity (or 'interweaving'), engagement and sensory enhancement. The interweaving here relates to the active engagement with a scriptural passage and deep reflection on how it relates to one's own life: '[It] blurs the boundary between what is external and what is within; between what is real in the world and what is imagined through the scriptures' (Luhrmann, 2013, p.713). As in the case of meditation, particularly forms of *samatha* practice described above, deep prayer involves absorption, or the 'capacity to become focused in a non-instrumental way on the mind's object—what humans imagine or see around them—and allow that focus to increase while diminishing one's attention to the myriad of everyday distractions that accompany the management of normal life' (ibid., p.711). Luhrmann measured levels of absorption among Christians attending a charismatic evangelical church (using the 'Tellegen Absorption Scale'), and concluded that those who had a high degree of absorption were those who were able to experience God most vividly, as a person, and to enter into a deep interactive relationship with that person.

Luhrmann argues that there are close parallels between what happens in the process of healing through prayer and the therapeutic practice of psychotherapists. Drawing on the work of D. W. Winnicott, she highlights the role of transitional objects which could represent to a child their mother's love in the absence of her physical presence. The mental construct created by this object has been defined by the psychoanalyst Heinz Kohut as a 'self-object' (Kohut, 2011). Self-objects are conceived of as a set of processes that provide vigour and cohesion to the self, based on the internalisation of these supportive, energising, organising, directive and regulatory functions, through there having been first performed consistently by others (Lovinger et al., 1999, p.271). The person who was helped by therapy was someone who acted, felt and thought as if they were always aware of the therapist's loving concern. The therapist becomes an ideal self-object: 'A sort of cross between a coach and a teddy bear, always available, never intrusive, whose emotional presence keeps hope alive and self-doubt at bay' (ibid., p.715). According to Luhrmann, through deep prayer, God can become that ideal self-object offering ongoing loving support to believers.

What is most striking is that Luhrmann has found evidence of the beneficial effects of prayer on mental health. The more spiritual statements people affirmed, she finds, the less lonely they were, the less stressed they felt, the more they experienced wellbeing and the higher satisfaction they had with life (measured by employing the 'Daily Spiritual Experiences Scale' developed by Lynn Underwood and Jeanne Teresi, along with a series of psychological rating scales, including the 'UCLA Loneliness Scale', the 'Perceived Stress Scale' and the 'Satisfaction with Life Scale'). The more they identified specifically with the statement, 'I feel God's love for me directly' (a statement that captures a sense of an imagined presence of God in their lives), the higher their scores on these mental health and wellbeing measures were. Luhrmann believes there is a significant relationship between deep prayer, a sense of closeness to God and mental health and wellbeing.

A further aspect of prayer that may enhance mental health and wellbeing is 'non-contact' healing, in which people pray for the recovery of others from illnesses or afflictions. This type of prayer is common practice in churches, where people routinely pray for the sick of the parish. One theory is that knowledge that others are praying for you actually positively affects the course of an illness. A recent meta-analysis of research findings indicates that even in circumstances where there is no knowledge of this healing activity, there are discernible impacts from prayer (Roe et al., 2015). Results further suggest that subjects exhibit a significant improvement in wellbeing relative to control subjects under circumstances that do not seem to be susceptible to placebo and expectancy effects. One recent study of 430 participants indicated that not all types of prayer were beneficial in terms of wellbeing. Those that were least beneficial were those that were ego-focussed and petitionary, whereas those that focussed outwardly on God had beneficial effects on wellbeing (ibid, 2015).

Practitioners in the mental health and wellbeing fields have demonstrated increasing interest in the therapeutic effects of prayer and the potential for integrating it into mental health services. Writing in the *Journal of Advanced Nursing*, Narayanasamy and Owens (2001) argue that, while the evidence for the healing power of prayer remains inconclusive, it is nevertheless felt to be beneficial by many patients and nurses, and that steps should be taken to explore how best to incorporate it into nursing practice. Therapists have also sought to examine ways to integrate prayer into psychotherapeutic practice, with studies having been undertaken into prayer's role in couples conflict, culturally competent care and addiction treatment, among others. As noted above in the work of Csordas, there is a range of ways in which counselling and psychotherapy may be integrated with prayer and religious healing. It should be noted too that prayer is an integral element in the lives of people of a variety of faiths, and while the extent to which it can cure illness or enhance mental health and wellbeing is still open to debate in scientific communities, for millions of religious people there is no doubt of its efficacy. The understanding of intercultural mental health and wellbeing therefore has to incorporate an appreciation of prayer in people's lives; including beliefs that it can change external circumstances or states of nature and that it can heighten a sense of subjective wellbeing. In this context, it is helpful to consider the position on religion and spirituality issued by the World Psychiatric Association:

World Psychiatric Association Position Statement on Spirituality and Religion

A tactful consideration of patients' religious beliefs and practices as well as their spirituality should routinely be considered and will sometimes be an essential component of psychiatric history taking.

An understanding of religion and spirituality and their relationship to the diagnosis, etiology and treatment of psychiatric disorders should be considered as essential components of both psychiatric training and continuing professional development.

There is a need for more research on both religion and spirituality in psychiatry, especially on their clinical applications. These studies should cover a wide diversity of cultural and geographical backgrounds.

The approach to religion and spirituality should be person-centered. Psychiatrists should not use their professional position for proselytizing for spiritual or secular worldviews. Psychiatrists should be expected always to respect and be sensitive to the spiritual/religious beliefs and practices of their patients, and of the families and carers of their patients.

Psychiatrists, whatever their personal beliefs, should be willing to work with leaders/members of faith communities, chaplains and pastoral workers, and others in the community, in support of the well-being of their patients, and should encourage their multi-disciplinary colleagues to do likewise.

Psychiatrists should demonstrate awareness, respect and sensitivity to the important part that spirituality and religion play for many staff and volunteers in forming a vocation to work in the field of mental health care.

Psychiatrists should be knowledgeable concerning the potential for both benefit and harm of religious, spiritual and secular worldviews and practices and be willing to share this information in a critical but impartial way with the wider community in support of the promotion of health and well-being.

Source: WPA 2016

The therapeutic implications of religion and spirituality are also central to a wide range of mental health professions. In the UK, the Royal College of Psychiatry (RCOP) has a thriving special interest group on spirituality, with over 3,600 members. Among its activities, it offers continuing professional development training on, 'exploring spirituality with people who use mental health services'. It has held meditation workshops at RCOP meetings and programmes on mindfulness. At the time of writing it has a continuing professional development module on mindfulness under development (www.rcpsych.ac.uk/members/special-interest-groups/spirituality/about-us). One aspect of its work is to support a study on 'hearing voices', funded by the Wellcome Trust and led by researchers at Durham University. This ongoing research includes a significant element on hearing voices in spiritual and religious contexts, and the development of therapeutic approaches that engage respectfully with the religious and spiritual experiences that people ascribe to these experiences (www.dur.ac.uk/hearingthevoice/). These examples suggest a significant shift in respectful engagement with religious and spiritual beliefs and practices in the mental health sphere. The potential for new developments relating to this shift will be further considered below.

Anthropological studies of the healing process are replete with examples where EMs may be seen as moving between the realm of popular or folk beliefs and more mainstream medical understandings. The general practitioner (GP) and anthropologist Cecil Helman, in a celebrated paper entitled 'Feed a Cold and Starve a Fever' explored the way GPs working in an English suburb themselves employed folk idioms in discussing illnesses with their patients. Helman noted that, 'Remedies which cannot be scientifically and biomedically justified are nevertheless prescribed by the physicians to meet their patients' need to "make sense" of biomedical treatment in terms of their folk model of illness. At the interface between physician and patient, biomedical diagnoses and treatment are more "negotiable" than previously realised' (1978, p.107). The suggestion is that processes of diagnosis should not simply be seen in terms of the imposition of an EM but as a complex negotiation in the doctor or healer seeks to make sense of the patient's/supplicant's problem through employment of idioms consistent with their religious or cultural frame of reference.

We note above that, in a term used by Csordas, illness or affliction may be 'remythologised' in the therapeutic process. The implication here is that, in the healing process there may be a movement from one view of the cause of a problem or affliction to another. A patient, for example, may be experiencing insomnia and, following consultation with a doctor, learn that they have depression, or some other psychological or physical diagnosis. Depending on the nature of the healer and the EM that they have been trained in, the condition may be understood in terms of unhealthy lifestyle, sin, familial conflicts or intrapsychic conflict. Some forms of diagnosis will engender family and community understanding and support, while others may result in incomprehension and ostracism. Given the importance of understanding, social engagement and support in recovery, the way in which an illness or affliction is represented can have considerable consequences for the individual's wellbeing. Diagnosing someone with a mental health problem can, in many cultural contexts, be highly stigmatising and result in less community support than may have been present if the problem has been placed within a more familiar and comprehensible cultural context. In doing so, careful consideration and discernment must be exercised on the impact of social and cultural factors, while avoiding simplistic and essentialist views of the impact of culture on an individual. As Rober and De Haene observe in relation to intercultural therapy: 'The underlying assumption is frequently that members of the same group will share the same cultural essence in terms of core practices and beliefs and that this essence would carry explanatory weight ... However, cultures are not things out there, with an essence to be described' (2014, p.7).

A further consideration is the role of power relations in healing and in the diagnostic process. The patients attending Helman's suburban clinic may have been negotiated with because they were seen as articulate and middle-class. In other circumstances, it may be that the GP negotiates meaning because she or he thinks that the patient may not understand the biomedical framing of their problem. In a relatively early contribution to the emerging field of transcultural psychiatry in the UK, Philip Rack (1982) talked about the way in which patients from ethnic minority groups may present 'pitfalls' in the recognition of psychiatric disorders, such as the presentation of somatic problems (for example a 'sinking heart') when they may be, in reality, suffering from depression. The psychiatrist Julian Leff (1973, 1988) argued that the languages of ethnic minorities may not have sufficient breadth to incorporate an appropriate vocabulary for psychiatric problems. I have previously offered a critique of these perspectives, pointing out that emphasis on the somatic is not, as implied, some form of masking or inarticulacy in expressing mental health problems. From my own research on South Asians interaction with mental health services, South Asian patients, rather than somatising, may readily and explicitly express a link between psychological, emotional and bodily states (Watters, 1996).

According to Lipowski, somatisation is defined in circumstances where patients, 'do not recognise, and may explicitly deny, a causal link between their distress and its presumed source' (1988, p.1359). The apparent somatisation of South Asians is not a product of South Asian 'culture' but rather of the context in which they receive treatment. It may be that doctors and therapists in Western biomedical traditions are unreceptive to ways in which emotional problems register at somatic levels (Watters, 2001). Rather than seeing the body and mind as operating holistically, Western models have often located problems within the realm of the mind, while not being receptive to corresponding effects on the body. Exclusive attention to somatic or psychological levels of distress may inhibit the potential for offering holistic forms of healing. However, recently emerging therapeutic perspectives like psychoneuroimmunology and mindfulness (in a Western clinical context) point to the dynamic interrelationships between body, mind and emotions, and provide new paradigms for viewing diagnostic and healing processes (Watters, 2001). These approaches will be considered further below.

Moreover, the quest for healing has often been shown to be a pragmatic one, in which people move between medical systems seeking relief for their symptoms and possible cures for their illnesses. In anthropological accounts of the use of medical systems around the world, the observation is often made that religious or folk traditions of medicine may coexist in relative harmony with forms of Western biomedicine. For example, in her extensive studies of the culture and experiences of mental illness, Jenkins points out that much anthropological evidence indicates that, 'people do not appear to be troubled by incommensurability or contradiction between alternative practices and systems'. She goes on to argue that, 'the idea that patients in a specialty mental health clinic might not without conflict or contradiction seek help from spiritual sources should be no more remarkable than the idea that trained physicians and mental health professionals might also be devout churchgoers' (Jenkins, 2015, p.204). Amarasingham (1980) has described the way in which people seeking cures may navigate between different medical systems in a pragmatic way, unperturbed by the apparent contradictions between differing views of the psyche and physiology which may underpin the systems that they use. These accounts suggest that an overriding concern is simply 'what works', rather than a preoccupation with potential incompatibilities between systems. Accounts of what I will refer to as 'healing journeys' also can reveal carefully calibrated ways in which people may use a combination of medical systems that may be seen to respond to different aspects of their problems.

The quest for healing: Chinese medicine

The English provincial city that has been a focus of my fieldwork over the past three years hosts a number of practitioners of traditional Chinese medicine (TCM). TCM includes all types of acupuncture (needle acupuncture, electric acupuncture, laser acupuncture, acupressure), *tuina* (i.e., Chinese massage at 'acupoints') and moxibustion (Wong, 2009, p.454). In one thriving practice, close to a local hospital, a number of doctors and other healthcare practitioners are regular patients and may be offered a range of treatments including acupuncture, acupressure, moxibustion, massage, herbal medicines and advice on lifestyle and diet. Consultations typically involve reading the pulse and blood pressure, inspecting the tongue, observing general demeanour and asking a series of questions on lifestyle and general wellbeing. Physiological, psychological and emotional issues are treated in an integrated and holistic manner. Unlike typical consultations with Western GPs, there is relatively little explicit focus on diagnosis. The patient often presents with a diagnosis received from their doctor or a specialist at the local hospital, and may already be on a regimen of drug treatments, but they are seeking a way of reducing symptoms and enhancing overall wellbeing. An observation from a study of a TCM practice in New York City is consistent with my own findings: 'One of the striking features of the patients' attitudes toward Chinese medical treatment in this study was the degree to which efficacy was not necessarily defined as cure. For example, in three cases in which Chinese medicine was not effective for the patient's presenting symptom, respondents spoke highly of the time, nurturing, and attention they had received from the practitioner' (Hare, 1993, p.34).

Consultations tend to be brisk, but are sharply focussed on key questions relating to known health problems, diet, mood and lifestyle. Practical steps may be suggested in terms of specific problems such as excessive alcohol consumption, smoking and use of illegal drugs. While I was unable to do a comprehensive study of the backgrounds of patients, my impression from numerous visits over approximately five years is that they were from a wide range of ethnic and social backgrounds, including African and Caribbean British, Indian British, Chinese and white English, and included middle-class and working-class backgrounds. The problems people sought help with ranged from long-term chronic health conditions to depression, general fatigue, high blood pressure or stress, as well as a wide range of diagnosed and undiagnosed conditions, including autistic conditions.

Consistent with the above observations regarding healing journeys and the fluidity of medical systems, patients would move seamlessly between TCM treatments and conventional Western medicine. The TCM doctor adopted a pragmatic approach to the presenting complaints. Where he thought appropriate, he would direct the patient to the hospital for assessment and treatment, and adopt a supporting role in the overall building of strength and wellbeing, often through a combination of acupuncture, acupressure and massage, along with herbal medicines. Diet was considered carefully, with recommendations often made to drink more water and green tea and have several small meals a day rather than one heavy meal in the evening. This overall interest in the wellbeing and empathic response of the TCM doctor is appreciated widely among those who use TCM. Hare, in her study of a TCM practice in New York also notes, 'the patient experienced both excellent medical results and an empathic relationship with his doctor that led him to change unhealthful behaviours, including an addiction to tranquilizers' (Hare, 1993, p.36).

Exercise 3.2 The Explanatory Models Approach

Example

It is interesting to reflect further on the healing journeys described above in the light of the widespread view of healing as involving a negotiation between explanatory models (EMs). With respect to the latter, the language of EMs is now widely incorporated into medical training in the US and UK, with clinicians encouraged to use the following series of questions in consultations with patients:

> Kleinman and colleagues have stressed the importance of engaging with the EMs of patients within mental health services.
> Key questions that may be used to explore the EMs of clients are as follows:
> What do you call this problem?
> What do you believe is the cause of this problem?
> What course do you expect it to take? How serious is it?
> What do you think this problem does inside your body?
> How does it affect your body and your mind?
> What do you most fear about this condition?
> What do you most fear about the treatment?

source: Kleinman (1988a)

Exercise

Consider how these questions may be applied in mental health settings. How do you think they may impact on the relationship between client/patient and mental health professional? What practical and organisational challenges may incorporation of EMs present?

Kleinman and Benson cautions that the use of EMs should be a means of opening a conversation with patients and should be done with an attitude of openness and sensitivity. Poor practice has been noted at times in the use of the approach, with clinicians using it in a technical diagnostic manner: 'The moment when the human experience of illness is recast into technical disease categories something crucial to the experience is lost because it was not validated as an appropriate clinical concern' (Kleinman and Benson, 2016 p.1674). The model suggests an egalitarian relationship between doctor and patient and, in some instances, it has been noted that members of particular cultural minorities and social groups may be uncomfortable with this approach. A Western-trained doctor may be sought out in the expectation of a more hierarchical relationship, in which the doctor will tell the patient what their problem is and what should be done about it without seeking the patient's own interpretations (see e.g. de Freitas 2011).

A wider issue, beyond that of the application of the interview, is how the concept of EMs may work in practice in diverse healing contexts. The healer – whether shaman, faith healer, traditional Chinese medicine practitioner, Western-trained doctor or psychologist – will usually work within formalised settings, in which time is carefully managed and the space in which healing occurs is resonant with images and paraphernalia indicative of the sovereignty of the model that will be applied. Patients' responses are likely to be affected by their prior understandings and the choice made to approach this particular type of healer, and the setting in which they enter will reinforce the sovereignty of the model to be used in that context.

Case Study: The Impact of Context and Power Relations on Enabling or Restraining Expression of Cultural Choices in Healing

An example from my own fieldnotes from research with Gujarati patients in London may serve as an example:

In my early years as a research student, I was asked by two anthropologists to help them with a research project on the extent to which traditional Hindu Ayurvedic medicine was used among Gujaratis in the UK. The research was to be conducted in Newham General Hospital in London, an area with a high concentration of black and minority ethnic people. My job was to work with the anthropologists to identify from the names of patients those whose family origins could be traced to Gujarat, and to undertake an interview with them about their use of Ayurvedic medicine. To facilitate my movement through the hospital I was given a name tag, white coat and clipboard. In the course of my interviews, I was surprised that hardly any patients indicated that they used Ayurvedic medicine.

When I reflected further after the interviews, I noted a discomfort and puzzlement among the patients when asked these questions. I detected a concern that the process of treatment may be compromised if Western-trained doctors had information that they were not adhering fully to a biomedical model of treatment. My formal questions and attire only exacerbated a sense of power imbalance with the patients as I stood by their bedsides. My concern that the results of the study may have been compromised by the institutional setting and style of interviewing was confirmed when I later undertook ethnographic fieldwork with Gujaratis in the same part of London. I met some of the people patients or relatives of patients who I had met in hospital. I was attending informal social events, worship at Hindu temples, caste gatherings, political events and weddings, even working briefly for a Gujarati newspaper. During the time I found that Ayurvedic medicine was widely used in the community, including by people who had professed ignorance of it in hospital.

This experience recorded above points to the importance of context, including quality of relationship and institutional and informal environments, in influencing self-expression of patients/clients. A further example occurred years later, when undertaking a series of interviews with asylum seekers as part of an evaluation of a mental health project for asylum seekers and refugees. Interviews were held in the offices of a major London-based NGO. Small interview rooms were allocated, furnished with just two or three chairs and a desk. The walls were blank and there were no windows. Clients would often arrive clutching a file of papers. Despite only living at subsistence level and in very precarious situations with respect to accommodation, every care would be taken to ensure that the papers were in good order. With often barely any time for introductions, the client would tell me their asylum story and emphasise their personal trustworthiness. Despite receiving prior advice from the service on the nature of the interviews, it generally took some time to convince the client that the purpose of the interview was to help evaluate a service that they were receiving and not to test the veracity of their asylum claims. At a later time, I undertook looser more ethnographic fieldwork with asylum seekers and noted how their narratives evolved into more candid accounts of their journeys and experiences (Watters, 2008).

In everyday interactions people demonstrate implicit awareness of the importance of place in constraining or enhancing the quality of communication. Offering to go for a coffee or have lunch with a new colleague indicates an interest in getting to know them outside of an office environment. Spaces for healing may provide information on models or practices that the patient may encounter in the healing processes, and on the qualifications of the practitioner. A TCM practitioner may have charts on the wall demonstrating the model used to understand the body and mind, including key energy points that are the focus for acupuncture and other treatment modalities. A counsellor or psychotherapist is likely to provide comfortable chairs to indicate the importance of relaxation and informality in the therapeutic session, certificates showing her qualifications and perhaps an array of books indicating her breadth of learning. A religious healer is highly likely to have symbolic objects in the treatment room – in the Christian traditions this might be a crucifix and perhaps statues of the Virgin Mary or certain saints. A British GP is likely to have charts on key activities to promote health, for example, concerning smoking, drinking or diet, as well as more discreet indications of linkages with pharmaceutical interventions and companies. The key point here is that EMs are reinforced by the physical environments. Treatments rarely take place in neutral spaces and practitioners have to consider carefully the messages they may be giving to patients. Within these spaces, patients may feel particularly constrained in articulating an alternative EM, as was the case with the Gujaratis who were interviewed about cultural-informed practices in the formal context of a Western hospital.

This chapter has illustrated the wide and disparate ways in which religion and spirituality intersect with understandings and practices aimed at enhancing mental health and wellbeing. Evidence points to a range of potentially beneficial linkages, from the impact of religious participation in enhancing social capital, to religious and spiritual practices themselves, such as prayer and meditation. We have noted the ways in which practices linking spirituality, religion and wellbeing may be underpinned by distinctive views of the interrelationships of mind, body and 'soul' or 'spirit' but how these may be navigated by people seeking healing. We note too how professional associations are seeking to engage with religion and spirituality to better understand the world views and explanatory models of patients and, also, to identify practices that may be incorporated into wider therapeutic programmes.

Part 2

THE CHANGING LANDSCAPE OF SERVICES

4 Rethinking Culture in Mental Health and Wellbeing

Chapter Overview

- An adapted acculturation model can be helpful in examining modalities of service provision within multicultural contexts.

- Multiculturalism and anti-racism have provided important insights into strengths and limitations of services aimed at enhancing mental health and/or wellbeing.

- A key challenge is to ensure people from diverse cultural groups have opportunities to define their own cultures and what these mean to them. This can help to avoid well-meaning but misguided attempts to provide services that are culturally sensitive.

In this section of the book we shift from an orientation towards exploring concepts and theories to one that is more practice-based. In doing so it is helpful to highlight key points from Part 1. Firstly, the contemporary world is 'on the move' in unprecedented ways, both in scale and diversity of migration. However, this movement is not only characterised by the scale and diversity of people moving from one country to another but also by mobility, both in terms of physical movement and ideas. In contemporary Europe, for example, people move between countries for work or leisure without committing to depart one country and live in another. The pace, scale and diversity of migration is accompanied by an increasingly rapid flow and exchange of ideas between countries and communities, resulting in an ever more dynamic environment in which people reflect on and develop ways of enhancing mental health and wellbeing. With respect to migration, the overarching paradigms that inform wider societal responses to migration and diversity conditions the way in which services towards migrants and refugees are designed and implemented. We are also faced with the spectre of large scale forced migration and of countries closing doors to external migrants at a time of grave humanitarian crisis. One face of migration is the relaxed cosmopolitanism of people who experience different environments and cultures as part of their lifestyles while another face is the plight of the refugee and undocumented migrant queueing in barren destitute areas, experiencing 'bare life' (Agamben, 1998), unwelcome and without citizenship.

Besides physical movement, as we have noted, there is a rapid movement of ideas, cultures and modes of expression, from musical forms, fashion, food, art and architectural styles, to cosmopolitan ideas about what constitutes the 'good life'. A glance at social media or newspapers reveals culturally diverse perspectives on what contributes to wellbeing. At the time of writing, the prominent British daily newspaper *The Times* carries a front-page story on how a 'Mediterranean diet' cuts male impotency by 40% (The Times, 30th August 2018). Inside the newspaper, advice for living well and improving concentration includes the – originally Buddhist (and on some accounts pre-Buddhist) – practice of mindfulness of the breath (*anapanasati*). Meanwhile in the same month, another major British newspaper, *the Guardian*, carried a cover feature on 'Mindfulness and Sex'. The journalist Emine Saner comments on the potential of mindfulness, 'It has been used by the NHS as a treatment for recurrent depression and popular books and apps have made it part of many peoples everyday lives. After mindful eating, drinking, parenting and working, mindful lovemaking is starting to be recognised more widely as a way to improve one's sex life' (Guardian 28th August 2018).

Increasingly people are incorporating ideas and practices formed in one cultural context into another. In the process, these ideas and practices – what I refer to as cultural modalities – are often adapted. While Berry introduced his framework for acculturation to focus on identity and interaction between groups in societies, some elements of the framework are also helpful in considering ideas and practices that travel from one context to another. Some ideas, for example, may be said to have been *assimilated* – in the sense that their cultural roots are ignored or obscured. Other practices are kept distinct from the mainstream. They coexist but are not incorporated into the landscape of services aimed at enhancing mental health and wellbeing. This may be because they are considered particularly esoteric and/or unscientific. A distinction may be made in this sense between mindfulness and shamanism. As we will go on to show, mindfulness has been embraced by a range of mainstream public bodies and has enthusiastic advocates within influential political and health service contexts. Shamanism doesn't have this level of support and is generally regarded as a tolerated but rather unusual approach more often associated with traditional tribal practices. The concept of marginalisation is also helpful here in pointing to practices that may be shunned in certain countries and communities. While not necessarily illegal, they may be seen as particularly dubious and potentially harmful practices, and their practitioners as manipulative and exploitative. Practices associated with the Church of Scientology, such as their programmes for treating drug and alcohol abuse, may be seen as good examples of this. One salient question is the extent to which the obscuring of cultural roots may be a necessary prerequisite to incorporation into mainstream services and, further, whether something may be lost in detaching a practice from its cultural context.

It is helpful to map the location and pervasiveness of intercultural models and approaches to mental health and wellbeing by drawing on Kleinman's model of a healthcare system as comprising of a popular (lay) sector, a folk sector and a professionalised sector . As noted in the examples we have considered, people can be seen as behaving in pragmatic and strategic ways in seeking help for their problems, and often combine elements from different sectors. The healthcare system itself can be seen as dynamically intercultural, with each sector incorporating differing cultural perspectives on understanding and treating illnesses and enhancing wellbeing. In the professionalised sector – which, in a British context, includes the NHS – one can see a dynamic incorporation of some treatment modalities from a range of sectors.

Diversity and the service environment: assimilation, multiculturalism and anti-racism

We have examined a number of ways of theorising and researching the impact of cultural diversity on wellbeing and mental health, including through studying social capital, acculturation and the capabilities approach, and the role of religion and culture in healing processes. As indicated, in this part of the book we consider how these developments in population mobility and diversity manifest in the spheres of mental health and wellbeing practices. It may be helpful initially to briefly sketch how diversity has been responded to in terms of research and policy, as this will help locate the place of mental health and wellbeing-oriented services. The primary example used is from the recent history of the UK, although salient differences with other countries will be noted where appropriate. A broad chronology in terms of the development of research and service paradigms is sketched below, from the 1970s through to the present day. In doing so it should be noted that one paradigm doesn't necessarily disappear when another arises. The multiculturalism that emerged in the 1970s is still with us, as is the assimilationist paradigm. Indeed, particularly in the wake of 9/11 there is evidence of assimilationism growing in strength across Europe and North America. Anti-racism remains a potent perspective both in academic research and public policy, with notable recent contributions in the mental health sphere (see for example Fernando, 2017).

The dominant paradigm in Britain prior to the 1970s was one of assimilation. In the wake of large-scale immigration from former colonies after the end of the second world war, there was an overriding emphasis on the importance of migrants 'adapting to our way of life'.

This emphasis was underpinned by a view of core British culture as relatively unchanging, with shared cultural values across all sections of the population. The duty of immigrants was to adapt to these values and relinquish, or at least not make overt displays of, their cultural differences. In this context, immigrants faced the prospect of leaving behind their past, and even if assimilation was sought, of feeling rejected by the host society. As V.S. Naipal remarked, 'Racial equality and assimilation are attractive but only underline the loss, since to accept assimilation is in a way to accept permanent inferiority' (Prospect, 1998). Sociological and anthropological studies in the 1970s and 1980s noted that, far from assimilating, cultural forms were proving highly durable and even being renewed and strengthened in succeeding generations of immigrant families. The 1970s witnessed an emergence of multiculturalism, particularly in the sphere of education. Rather than suggesting that ethnic minorities in the UK should assimilate, an emphasis was placed on the celebration of cultural diversity, with school students learning about different religious and cultural traditions in the UK and being encouraged towards building an understanding of different cultures. This approach was roundly criticised by some commentators, including the present author, for promoting naïve representations that, rather than combat discrimination, may reinforce it by emphasising the otherness of ethnic groups (Watters, 1996).

A further powerful strand of criticism pointed to the way in which racial discrimination was not addressed by multicultural approaches. As informed by multiculturalism, society was often represented as consisting of a kind of mosaic of ethnic groups with their distinctive cultures without addressing power imbalances between groups. One commentator memorably described multiculturalism as concerned with 'steel bands, saris and samosas' (Modood and May, 2001) while paying little attention to underlying inequalities and discrimination. Multiculturalism itself was increasingly seen as a manifestation of a ubiquitous racism in British institutions, that acted to deny the lived experience of discrimination of black people in Britain. One influential volume entitled *The Empire Strikes Back* published in 1982 directly attacked the influence of multiculturalism in Britain. According to one of its authors (commenting on the ways in which Asian people were portrayed in multiculturalism): 'These representations are influential in defining "problems" which are associated with Asian people and are shared by local government, the health service, the youth service and the social services', and, as such, 'predetermine the parameters of activity by a range of welfare agencies' (Lawrence, 1982, p.134). An alternative anti-racist approach was advocated that directly addressed institutional racism oriented towards challenging discrimination against black people.

Anti-racism itself has been criticised not least because of evidence of significant disparities in educational and economic achievement between black and minority ethnic (BAME) groups, and further that, as noted above, on a number of substantive indicators, some black and minority ethnic (BAME) groups were actually doing better than the native population in terms for example of access to prestigious professions, income levels and educational achievement (GovUK 2019, IPPR, 2007). This has challenged the portrayal of black and minority ethnic (BAME) groups as uniformly subject to discrimination and indicated that a more nuanced approach to researching different groups was timely. While each of these approaches may be seen to have arisen in recognition of the of limitations in what were previously dominant paradigms, none of these approaches has disappeared and, in the present context, continue to influence the sphere of academic research, policy and practice in mental health and wellbeing. The orientation of services is crucially under-pinned by these paradigms, from a 'one size fits all' approach that assumes that, whatever the cultural background of the client or patient, it is their job to adapt to services, to a multicultural approach that seeks to reflect community diversity in the way services are shaped and delivered. An anti-racist approach may be seen in services that seek to address perceived power imbalances rooted in racism.

A problem with both multiculturalism and anti-racism is that they both in effect may act to homogenise black and ethnic minority communities. In the case of anti-racism this may be manifest in arguing that members of black and ethnic minority groups have shared identities through experincing ubiquitous discrimination. Multiculturalism informs a devel-opment of services that are specific to perceived cultural needs and preferences but can rest on a series of 'common sense assumptions' about what the problems in a particular community or group may be. As I have described elsewhere, South Asian women in one locality were perceived to suffer from high levels of depression, not based on epidemio-logical surveys but on a general perception that this was the case (Watters, 1996).

Exercise 4.1

Example

The example concerns a middle aged South Asian man with a history of mental health problems. His South Asian community psychiatric nurse suggested that Ravi may wish to attend the Asian drop-in group, but the latter said he had no wish to attend an "Asians only group". He did instead begin to regularly attend a day centre for homeless people run by a voluntary agency in the inner city, where he began to undertake a number of practical activities including cooking. At the time I completed field work, it was difficult to judge the extent to which regular counselling by the Asian worker was going to have a positive outcome for Ravi. He had, as I have noted, no desire to participate in activi-ties designed specifically for Asian clients. He felt rejected by his family, and a failure because of his difficulties in employment; he had no ongoing links with any members of the Asian communities in the city or, indeed, with any other groups. He was an intel-ligent and articulate man, and when pushed would argue strongly that the way he chose to live was a rational decision based on what he perceived to be the worthlessness of his life. He was often very antagonistic to the interventions of psychiatric workers who he regarded as intruding on his freedom and, at times, as giving him medication under false pretences. The South Asian community psychiatric nurse felt that, given Ravi's disposition, it may be effective to challenge some of the views on which he based his lifestyle. The fact that, following a period of counselling, Ravi participated in some day centre activity, particularly involvement in the preparation of food, was viewed by the community mental health team as suggesting that he may have taken some small steps towards recovery.

An inconvenient truth in the same locality was that South Asian men often suffered from drug and alcohol problems but this was not referred to by community leaders when service providers sought to map health needs in the area. South Asian women who did present with depression or anxiety were often suffering from the stress of having a partner at home who was suffering from addiction problems. The broad point is that communities may have an investment in representing themselves in particular ways and these representations may obscure a range of problems the community may face. Where these are reinforced by the common sense assumptions of service providers, a situation can develop in which ingrained and durable services and service responses are generated that may miss something important in addressing the mental health needs of a community.

Exercise

Consider how service providers view this man's culture. What might constitute a culturally sensitive approach in this context? What are lessons for categorising people into cultural groups?

It is notable here that locating mental health patients within 'their' ascribed community was seen as having implicit therapeutic benefits. The day centre was established so that isolated South Asian women could share cultural activities such as cooking and handicrafts. However, for the mental health patient, community may be something that is seen as oppressive as it carries with it associations of having been stigmatised and falling short of expectations. A similar situation is noted below in which young refugees were assumed by social services to be most comfortable being placed near a mosque and cultural centre within an ethnically diverse locality. This however ignored the fact that they may find association with a familiar cultural group oppressive and that they may too have certain biases that made them uncomfortable mixing with a range of ethnic groups. This point has been echoed by the anthropologist Nigel Rapport who has argued that it is inappropriate to view leaving one's community as solely as source of suffering and loss (Rapport, 2006). Leaving a community can also be liberating and provide openings to forge new identities less encumbered by the views and opinions of those known previously. The pressures towards maintaining a cultural identity may come from community but also, as noted above, from services.

The navigation of perceived bridges between cultures in mental health care has given rise to a wealth of service initiatives aimed towards the development of 'cultural competency', 'cultural mediation', 'intercultural therapy' and 'cultural sensitivity'. A challenge of these approaches is that they can be reductive and function as a way of translating rich cultural accounts of illness or suffering into formulaic diagnostic categories. Moreover, issues that may be understood by patients as reflecting a problematic social or political context may be reinterpreted as individual problems. As I have previously observed in relation to the mental health care of refugees: 'Bilingual therapists thus operate within well-defined and circumscribed contexts. They listen to the stories of the refugees but they translate them in such a way that they can be operationalised as mental illness categories within a medical hierarchy. Thus, while the employment of people from similar ethnic and cultural backgrounds to the refugees themselves may be cited by services as evidence of cultural sensitivity, they may in fact be seen as agents of de-culturalisation and de-politicisation in that they transfigure the refugees' accounts into individualised pathology' (Watters, 2001, p.1712). An alternative approach, in the case of refugees, is highly practical and responsive to the range of needs a client may have within their present situation.

Exercise 4.2

Example

An example can be drawn here from the Bi-cultural Team based at the Refugee Council in London (Watters, 2007). Following an initial assessment of needs undertaken at the organisation's reception, those who appear to have mental health problems are referred to the team who undertake a more comprehensive assessment. On the basis of this, a range of approaches may be adopted. The team member may offer a series of counselling sessions combined with help with practical matters as well as providing a resource for ongoing contact. If the client appears to need help from other agencies there were a range of options for referral. Those who appear to have been victims of torture were referred to the Medical Foundation for the Care of Victims of Torture, who would offer an in-depth assessment and also a range of therapeutic options. Often clients would have a complex range of needs that were met by engaging with a variety of agencies involving, for example, making links with GPs, accommodation providers, legal support and possibly also schools and colleges. The model here recalls aspects of the integrated approach described by Silove and his colleagues at the University of New South Wales, as it incorporates both an aspect of direct psychosocial care provision as well as a capacity to offer outreach to a range of agencies (Silove et al., 1999)

Exercise

Consider the merits of this approach. What resources would service providers need to make it effective? How would assessments be undertaken? What challenges would there be in ensuring the approach was sustainable?

As Fernando has argued, a receptive approach involves asking those receiving services how they perceive their own cultures (Fernando, 2005). One could go further and suggest that besides this, clients and patients should be asked to share their views of what their community looks like, who they regard as family and what their understanding is of culture. Kareem and Littlewood, writing about the work of the intercultural therapy centre Nafsiyat, stressed the importance of challenging views and stereotypes by allowing patients to define their own cultural worlds (Kareem and Littlewood, 2000). Sourangshu Acharyya, one of the mental health professionals who established Nafsiyat described the approach as follows: 'Understanding the "culture" of patients includes taking into account both their personal experiences in the societies in which they were born and lived, the experience of the "migrant culture" of parents and grandparents, and the way of life created by minorities in British society to affirm and maintain their own identity, a way of life into which subsequent generations are born' (Acharyya et al., 1989, p.359). Rober and de Haene writing in the *Journal of Family Therapy*, add that the primary focus should be on the person in therapeutic encounters, not their presumed culture: 'People should not be seen as representatives of cultures, abstractions, but rather, as human beings actively producing culture in their attempts to lead life as best they can' (Rober and de Haene, 2014 p.9).

5 | The Role of Nature and Place in Mental Health and Wellbeing

Chapter Overview

- The Five Ways to Wellbeing are introduced.
- Evidence is presented demonstrating the links between exposure to, and engagement with, nature, and related improvements in mental health and wellbeing.
- Particular ethnic and cultural groups may feel inhibited or unwelcome in using the natural environment. It is important that these barriers are explored and addressed.
- Gardening- and nature-based therapeutic programmes may provide particular benefits to populations that have been uprooted, giving them a sense of place and belonging.
- The interrelationship between concern for the environment and wellbeing is further supported by recent research pointing to the compatibility of psychological and ecological wellbeing.
- Physical places are often associated with therapeutic properties. These may be locations in which there are shared community associations and narratives that are seen to enhance wisdom and wellbeing.

A starting point is to consider the advice of the NHS on mental wellbeing. The promotion of mental wellbeing is viewed as consisting of five 'ways to wellbeing'. It is notable that this core guidance on the development of mental wellbeing is viewed as involving engagement with the wider community through altruism, participation in classes and group events and connecting to neighbours. It is not rooted in a particular cultural domain and describes activities that are potentially meaningful to people from a wide range of ethnic or cultural backgrounds.

The Five Ways to Wellbeing

Connect – connect with the people around you: your family, friends, colleagues and neighbours. Spend time developing these relationships.

Be active – you don't have to go to the gym. Take a walk, go cycling or play a game of football. Find an activity that you enjoy and make it a part of your life.

Keep learning – learning new skills can give you a sense of achievement and a new confidence. So why not sign up for that cooking course, start learning to play a musical instrument, or figure out how to fix your bike?

Give to others – even the smallest act can count, whether it's a smile, a thank you or a kind word. Larger acts, such as volunteering at your local community centre, can improve your mental wellbeing and help you build new social networks.

Be mindful – be more aware of the present moment, including your thoughts and feelings, your body and the world around you. Some people call this awareness 'mindfulness'. It can positively change the way you feel about life and how you approach challenges.

Source: NHS Moodzone

While relatively simple and straightforward, these modalities are underpinned by, and are the product of, considerable empirical research. The exhortations to connect and learn new skills, for example, are supported by the literature on mental health and social capital, referred to above and by a considerable weight of evidence on the positive impact of 'the social cure' on mental health and general wellbeing. A key message from this literature is that participation in social activities enhances wellbeing to the extent that there is currently a growing movement towards 'social prescribing' in the UK. As a support to health promotion and recovery from illness, patients are being assigned to wellbeing workers who help them engage in a range of activities, from joining walking groups to clubs, yoga, sports activities and so on.

A key component of the new movement towards social prescribing is engagement of patients with natural environments. Jules Pretty, Professor of Environment and Society at the University of Essex, has pointed to the vital role that contact with nature plays in promoting mental health and wellbeing. Pretty makes the observation that nature can have an immunising effect on people by protecting from stresses in the future, it can help us recover problems and stresses in our lives and help us concentrate and think more clearly (Pretty et al., 2004, 2005). As Sternberg has pointed out, 'the notion that nature was important to healing has been around for thousands of years – going back to classical times, when temples to Asclepius, the Greek god of healing, were built far from towns, high on hilltops overlooking the sea' (Sternberg, 2009, p.3). In distilling the research evidence Pretty and his colleagues have discerned three levels at which nature may impact on mental and physical wellbeing:

Exercise 5.1

Example

1. The first is viewing nature, as through a window, or in a painting.
2. The second is being in the presence of nearby nature, which may be incidental to some other activity, such as walking or cycling to work, reading on a garden seat or talking to friends in a park.
3. The third is active participation and involvement with nature, such as gardening or farming, trekking or camping, cross-country running or horse riding.

(Pretty et al, 2005)

Exercise

Consider the extent to which it may be possible to introduce these three elements into a service you are familiar with.

A particular emphasis has been placed on recent research findings on the linkages between engagement with nature and social activities. In this context Pretty has pointed to the benefits of 'green exercise'. An optimal programme for promoting mental and physical wellbeing would be one in which exercise is taken by groups in natural environments and accompanied by a form of learning, for example, about wildlife in a local habitat. A key challenge resides in the fact that natural environments may not always been seen as accessible by people from different ethnic and cultural backgrounds or by those who are vulnerable, for example, owing to age and disability. The case study below illustrates a recent attempt to gain understanding of the barriers that may exist for different groups in society; in this instance focussing on a BAME group and elderly people living in supported housing.

Case Study: Nature Based Wellbeing Activities for Black and Minority Ethnic and Elderly Groups

In view of the research evidence in favour of the benefits of undertaking physical activities while in nature, there are compelling arguments in favour of encouraging access to green and open spaces for vulnerable sections of the population. In a preliminary study undertaken by the author, two groups in particular were identified: elderly people living in supported housing and members of black and minority ethnic (BAME) communities, living in the context of a largely homogeneous white English population. Both of these populations live in areas that border the South Downs National Park, a large national park in the southeast of England. Anecdotal local evidence suggested both groups were unlikely to use the Park.

In order to try and understand why, two focus groups were established to determine the attitude of the groups to the Park and these were coupled with events aimed at enhancing the groups' knowledge and appreciation of the facilities offered by the Park. Drawing on the information gathered in the focus groups and from a questionnaire, measures of the impact of the Park on vulnerable groups wellbeing were suggested.

The aim of the focus groups was to demonstrate the impact on health and wellbeing of access to the Park for black, ethnic minority and elderly peoples. This was a first step towards creating an evidence base for the impact on conditions for different groups of people in localities close to the Park, based on what they themselves see as important. Therefore, the proposed instrument was 'grounded' in that it drew directly on the perspectives of the people studied.

The following key questions were addressed to the groups:

1. How did you hear about the South Downs National Park?
2. Do you make use of the Park?
3. If so, what do you use the Park for?
4. If not, what prevents you from using the Park?
5. Is there anything specific that would help you make more use of the Park in the future?

The Question of Access

The most common reason given in both groups was having a lack of knowledge about the Park. This included not knowing how to access the Park and being unsure of its location. Many in the BAME group thought that access to the park was restricted. When asked to clarify 'restricted' the women spoke of not being sure if they were allowed to walk across fields unsupervised; whether you had to be professional walkers, whether you had to pay to access it or to have to belong to a club.

Another point raised was that of BAME communities not wanting to mix with other communities including other BAME communities. The reasons discussed included lifestyles of some BAME communities who tended to focus on staying indoors, relationships which were cultural based where men did not approve of women socialising outside family circles and communities lacking in self-confidence. Indeed, BAME men in this particular context were presented as generally averse to walking and more inclined to domestic and sedentary activities.

For the elderly group living in supported housing, the question of access was also linked to whether they would simply be able to walk in the Park, that is, whether the park had the equipment and physical resources to access the park. The importance of having an able and enthusiastic partner and/or friend was stressed by both groups. In one instance, a woman was married to a man who was an enthusiastic walker with a strong local knowledge. This was pivotal in helping her gain the confidence to go walking and to identify points of interest in the Park.

Specific Health Issues

The elderly group had some distinct self-reported heath issues associated with access to the Park. Many were overweight and had difficulty walking for anything more than short distances. They did however view the Park as providing opportunities for exercise that may offer a way to reduce their weight. They saw exercise in the Park as potentially part of a package of measures that could combine with dietary changes that would improve their health. Both the elderly and BAME groups also saw potential benefits in terms of mental and emotional health and were extremely positive about the way walking in nature could improve their moods and self-esteem. Going into the Park was associated with being 'calming', 'relaxing', 'making me feel better about myself', giving a chance to have some personal 'space' in which to connect with nature. It is important to note that walking in nature was perceived as being quite different to going to the gym, as the open space, fresh air and visual environment was seen to have benefits for mind and body.

Lack of self confidence

Both groups expressed some concerns about having self-confidence to go on walks and stressed the importance of group activity. The lack of self-confidence was explored further with the BAME women who commented on how they did not feel confident on their own to participate in activities and the importance of having support groups which enables them to venture outside their comfort zones and explore new opportunities. The local group the BAME women belonged to was clearly seen as a catalyst towards generating opportunities to go to the Park and members were encouraging of each other to explore the Park together.

Professionalizing of Walking

Some of the elderly and the BAME group had doubts about whether 'walking' was suitable for them. They spoke of the perceived need to own what was seen as expensive clothing and equipment in order to walk which was discouraging. The elderly group felt that it was often presented as something for younger people. In the BAME group 'walking' was seen by the majority of the women as a professional past time that needed specific equipment and knowledge and very much as belonging to the white middle classes. It is interesting that the question of entitlement to walk in the Park was less strongly expressed in the white elderly group, although access, in the sense of being physically able to go to the Park was a salient issue.

Both groups discussed what they would do to encourage communities to walk more.

> Everyone agreed the South Downs National Park needs to raise its profile. This should include clear information on the Parks and how to access them. The benefits on health from walking should be proactively promoted as well as challenging existing perceptions around walking – e.g. that you need to be professionally equipped in order to walk in the Parks.
>
> The importance of support groups was very strongly voiced. Most of the BAME women said they would not have taken part in any of the activities if they did not belong already to a BAME community group. One woman said she knew about the walks through her volunteering role with Sussex Community Development Association (SCDA) but agreed that support groups were very important.

Of course, proximity to a national park does not offer the only potential opportunity for engagement with nature. Gardening is a common activity in many countries and cultures, from suburban areas to urban city and roof gardens. Researchers, writing in the *Journal of Public Health*, have noted the particular mental health and wellbeing benefits of tending to allotments, a popular form of gardening in the UK. The researchers note that 'allotment gardeners have a better level of self-esteem and mood and a reduced level of abnormal psychological functioning than non-gardeners' (Wood et al., 2016, p.337). The authors argue that, 'in order to improve health and well-being, people in the UK should be encouraged to take part in short bouts of allotment gardening. Health organizations and policy makers should consider the potential of allotment gardening as long-term tool for combatting the increasing prevalence of ill-health and local public authorities should seek to provide community allotment plots to allow residents to have regular opportunities to partake in gardening activities' (Wood et al., 2016, p.342). Besides evidence of ways in which gardening activities may enhance the wellbeing of the general population, there is also increasing evidence that they may be particularly beneficial for migrant and refugee communities.

On a visit to refugee communities in Sydney, Australia in the late 1990s I was struck by a comment by a group from the former Yugoslavia, who said that one of the most difficult things for them in transitioning to Australia was 'the weather'. When I enquired further, the refugee said, 'at home we have seasons and in the countryside our lives revolve around growing and harvesting crops. Here there are no seasons. It is very disorientating'. This is an aspect of the refugee and migrant experience that has been given little attention until relatively recently. However, in recent years a variety of therapeutically oriented gardening projects have been introduced for migrants and refugees in a number of countries, including the UK, Australia and the USA. One study investigating the benefits of allotment gardening for refugees in the north of England used an ethnographic approach and employed observation, semi-structured interviews and photo-elicitation interviews. According to the researchers, 'Analysis revealed three themes: horticulture as a meaningful activity; a beneficial social environment and positive effects of occupational engagement. These themes were considered in the context of doing, being, belonging and becoming' (Bishop and Purcell, 2013, p.268). Horticulture represented a purposeful activity that brought people who had moved across the world in often dangerous, unpredictable and painful circumstances, into a sustained relationship with the soil and with a group of people in a new country. They learned new skills and applied those they already had to a new environment learning the subtleties of a new ecosystem and how to work with it in a fulfilling way. A similar project was undertaken in Australia with a group of African migrants and researchers had similar results that emphasised three themes: land tenure, reconnecting with agriculture, and community belonging. They concluded that, 'Community food gardens offer a tangible means for African refugees, and other vulnerable or marginalised populations, to build community and community connections. This is significant given the increasing recognition of the importance of social connectedness for wellbeing' (Harris et al., 2014, p.9202).

Besides the benefits of horticultural-based therapy for migrants and refugees, the wider issue of the importance of contact with nature in enhancing mental health and wellbeing offers an example of the way in which ideas from different cultural contexts have been incorporated into interventions and services. Recent research in Western countries on green exercise and the benefits of engagement with woodland is complemented by work in East Asia on the mental health and wellbeing benefits of spending time in forests. As Hansen and colleagues have noted: 'Research conducted in transcontinental Japan and China points to a plethora of positive health benefits for the human physiological and psychological systems associated with the practice of Shinrin-Yoku (SY), also known as Forest Bathing. Shinrin-Yoku is a traditional Japanese practice of immersing oneself in nature by mindfully using all five senses (Hansen et al., 2017, p.851).

A review by Yu and colleagues from the National Taiwan University illustrates that a short forest bathing program is a promising therapeutic method for enhancing heart rate and blood pressure functions as well as an effective psychological relaxation strategy for middle-aged and elderly individuals (Yu et al., 2017, p.897). In undertaking an in-depth review of salient literature, Hansen et al. note a wide range of studies demonstrating the benefits of both forest bathing and nature therapy for a range of physical and mental health conditions. In concluding their review they point out that substantial research evidence 'honors and supports the increased awareness of the positive health-related effects (e.g., stress reduction and increased holistic well-being) associated with humans spending time in nature, viewing nature scenes via video, being exposed to foliage and flowers indoors and the development of urban green spaces in large metropolitan areas worldwide' (Hansen, 2017, p.44). In the UK, the anthropologist Karis Petty has explored the benefits of contact with woodlands for people who suffer from visual impairments. In taking regular immersive walks in woodlands Petty notes a range of benefits that enhance wellbeing deriving from the aural and tactile landscape. Sensory engagement with the textures and sounds of the landscape while noting the interconnectedness of the natural environment, produces experiences that are both calming and uplifting for participants (Petty, 2017). The valuing of the natural environments is something found among people in different continents and across different classes. As Pretty notes in reviewing a wide range of international research evidence, 'Green space is important for mental well-being, and levels of use have been linked with longevity and decreased risk of mental ill-health in Japan, Scandinavia and the Netherlands' (Pretty, 2007, p.42).

Given the wide range of research findings from international quantitative and qualitative studies on the benefits for mental health and wellbeing derived from contact with the natural environment, Pretty and colleagues argue that the time has come for much more imaginative, substantial and sustained investment in this area. This comes at a time of unprecedented threats to the natural environment from, for example, climate change, unsustainable farming methods, deforestation and air pollution. Just as mindful and harmonious contact with the natural environment has significant benefits, so environmental neglect and degradation impacts negatively on mental health and wellbeing. Pretty et al. note that, just as images and engagement with the natural environment can enhance the benefits of green exercise, images of environmental degradation can diminish and reverse the mental health benefits of exercise. This is particularly acute in relation to the impact of images showing despoiling of the countryside with these having a greater effect than images of urban decay. They note that, 'The rural unpleasant scenes had the most dramatic effect, depressing the beneficial effects of exercise on three different measures of mood. It appears that threats to the countryside depicted in rural unpleasant scenes have a greater negative effect on mood than already unpleasant urban scenes' (Pretty et al., 2005, p.319).

There is a wide range of research evidence of the direct impact of environmental damage on both physical and mental health. Researchers from three Canadian universities documented the mental health impact on climate change on indigenous communities in Labrador. They concluded that climate change was negatively impacting mental health and wellbeing due to 'disruptions in land-based activities and a loss of place-based solace and cultural identity'. They added that, 'Participants reported that changes in climate and environment increased family stress, enhanced the possibility of increased drug and alcohol usage, amplified previous traumas and mental health stressors, and were implicated in increased potential for suicide ideation' (Willcox 2013 p.255, Cunsolo et al., 2012). Air pollution has been shown in a number of studies to impair brain functioning and reduce people's sense of wellbeing. Zhang et al., for example, report that: 'By making use of variations in exposure to air pollution for the same individuals over time, we show that air pollution reduces hedonic happiness and increases the rate of depressive symptoms' (2017, p.81). The global breadth of the problem and the shared human value placed on the natural environment, suggests that taking measures that harness good practice in various parts of the world is both essential and urgent. Scholars and practitioners are, at the time of writing, forming new theoretical models and agendas for action that attempt to link perspectives on engagement with nature with improvements in mental health and wellbeing. These include programmes aimed at people with mental health problems offering active engagements with the natural environment (Shimmin et al., 2018, Adams and Morgan, 2016). This interrelationship between concern for the environment and wellbeing is further supported by recent research pointing to the compatibility of psychological and ecological wellbeing. The psychologists Brown and Kasser have noted complementarity between subjective wellbeing (SWB) and ecologically responsible behaviour (ERB). They note that an intrinsic value system and disposition towards the practice of mindfulness were related to both SWB and ERB while a life of voluntary simplicity was related to ERB (Brown and Kasser, 2005).

Green Mind Theory – proposed by Jules Pretty and colleagues at the University of Essex – represents an emerging paradigm in the field. It builds upon interconnected, interdisciplinary and intercultural research on green exercise and nature-based therapies, incorporating understanding derived from neuroscience and brain plasticity, spiritual and wisdom traditions, the lifeways of original cultures and material consumption behaviours (Pretty, 2017). It builds too on a world view of radical interconnectedness, in which the body, mind and environment all require integration in order to generate mental health and wellbeing. It is underpinned by a perspective in which focus on techniques to improve the body and mind alone are insufficient if they do not also cultivate awareness of the natural environment and develop modes of action that enhances rather than diminishes or destroys the natural environment. The Buddhist teacher and environmental activist Thannisara argues that engagement with environmental issues is an essential part of a spiritual path: 'Everything is now changing very fast. Our personal journeys are intersecting with a global evolutionary arc of colossal proportions. We are awakening into the realization that our special, personal enlightenment treks ... are not going to inspire the kind of "game changer" needed to ensure a sustainable planet for future generations' (Thanissara, 2015, p.2). The linkage between personal wellbeing and positive engagements with the environment is also advocated by Teresa Belton who argues that human and environmental health are inextricably linked: 'The prescriptions of psychologists and others who have codified the foundations of wellbeing have completely neglected to consider the inbuilt need of human beings to have contact with the natural world, which is, after all, the environment in which our species has evolved and in which we are therefore at home. This missing element is crucial because it unites the two issues of human wellbeing and environmental sustainability' (Belton, 2014 kindle location 5070).

As noted, there is a growing wealth of research evidence demonstrating the mental health and wellbeing benefits of being in natural environments. These include simply being in, and appreciating, these environments through the senses, to doing specific activities within them, in the form of green exercise, horticulture or activities aimed towards environmental protection and sustainability. These practices can help ground populations who have been on the move and make displaced people feel they have a role as custodians in new environments. Horticultural therapeutic activities are employed, for example, by Freedom from Torture, a long-established British NGO that works primarily with refugees who have fled their homelands (freedomfromtorture.org). The orientation towards therapeutic engagement with nature is often referred to as ecotherapy and this underpins a growing range of services for people with mental health problems. The 'Grow Project' in the south east of England, for example, offers a programme of eight weekly sessions over a season for people with conditions such as depression, anxiety, stress and other 'moderate' mental health problems. Participants are able to choose from a wide range of nature-based activities including guided nature walks, conservation tasks, green woodworking, wild food foraging, beach-combing, shepherding, mindfulness and creative activities.

An evaluation by the University of Brighton pointed to the effectiveness of the programme in alleviating mental health symptoms and enhancing wellbeing. Findings indicated that benefits of ecotherapy included: positivity, nature connectedness, autonomy, belonging and improved sense of social identity. The programme appeared to also have longer term impacts: '77% reported they were learning or developing practical skills since taking part with 74% of participants reporting that they had engaged with either volunteering, work, training or education following their participation in Grow' (Adams and Morgan, 2016, p.13). Besides the beneficial effects of being in nature and engaging with it in appreciative and practical ways, the UK mental health charity MIND notes that ecotherapy can include animal-assisted therapy, structured programmes of farming and outdoor activities such as rock climbing and rafting (MIND, 2018).

Healing places

A further consideration here is of the role certain places may play in the process of healing. Religious traditions have a wide array of places that are associated with the sacred and these are often sites of pilgrimage for people suffering from a range of afflictions. Lourdes in southern France is one example where, since a peasant girl experienced an apparition believed to be the Virgin Mary in 1858, some 200 million people are estimated to have visited the village. The river Ganges in India is a sacred site of healing where millions bath every year at auspicious times and locations, most notably at Varanasi. As the Harvard Indologist Diana Eck notes, in Hinduism, the Ganges is seen as both goddess and river and its waters are seen as the liquid embodiment of *shakti*, female spiritual power as well as the sustaining immortal fluid of mother's milk (Eck, 2011. For Hindus, bathing in the Ganges is thought to hold the potential for realising a range of benefits, from relief from poverty and bad dreams to ultimate spiritual liberation, *moksha*, or release from the bondage of the world (Bowker, 1970, p.118).

Places, as such, may be seen as particularly auspicious, offering the potential for cures for mental and physical afflictions. These cures may be realised even if the person suffering is not present. The anthropologist Veda Skultans examined the role of a healing temple in Maharashtra in India and noted that it was a site where women would go often to pursue healing for children – normally sons – or husbands afflicted by mental illness. Through their devotions, they sought to transfer their sons' illness to themselves and thereby cure their child. Skultans notes that, 'Women come as care givers accompanying a mentally ill family member. But although they arrive as care givers and, indeed, continue to fulfil that function, they become afflicted by trance soon after their arrival. Women see this transformation into patienthood as resulting from their devotion to their families. Indeed, they pray that the illness be transferred from their sons, husband or daughters to themselves' (Skultans, 1987, p.661). In this instance, a quality of the place itself helps induce the trance and creates a possibility of healing for the child or husband through relocation of the disorder.

In Joao Pessoa in the north-east of Brazil, an annex to a church has a room filled with replicas of parts of the body that are believed to have been cured by the intercession of the Virgin Mary. The healing powers of the location were said to have dated from 1763 when a Dutch ship was trying to dock in the midst of a ferocious storm. The captain and crew made a promise that if, through the intercession of the Virgin Mother they were allowed to dock safely, they would build a church in the location. The church was subsequently built and the idea that this was a particularly auspicious place where promises could be made in return for divine help, continued to grow. Every year thousands of people come to the church and offer a replica, or something closely associated with something or someone they wish to be healed. In 2011 I undertook interviews with Brazilians who used the church and who had donated items. Some had come to ask for help to have successful pregnancies and had subsequently offered photos of their babies with messages of thanks on the back. Some brought replicas of limbs they wished to have healed, for example, the cast of a knee. In one instance, a man brought photos of bullet wounds that were going to be operated on. After receiving a successful resolution for a mental health problem, a man had brought a replica of his head that he had carved out of wood. The priest who undertook services at the church did not discourage the practice but did not accept the view that healing was a transactional matter. He said people's cures were a consequence of their faith and not of the particular promises they made.

The distinction made by the priest is one that is arguably central to differentiating between religion and magic and is of fundamental importance in understanding the role of religious and lay understandings of processes of healing. Jan de Vries, a pioneering scholar in the study of religions presented the relationship between religion and magic as a site of conflict: 'Time and again magic threatens to trespass against religion; time and again man's attitude may change from respectful worship into the desire to coerce and govern. Even in Christianity the holiest acts are not safe from sliding towards and abuse by magic' (de Vries, 1962, p.214). However, investigations of the places where people seek healing often gives rise to a sense of the coexistence and interpenetration of religious traditions and so-called magical practices. Healing places combine a sense of reverence and veneration with a sense that the mundane earthly realm can be transfigured through pious acts in sites imbued with spirituality. The ultimate spiritual goal may be one in which the things of this world are cast aside but, for many, healing places offer a chance to alleviate and change the direction of worldly afflictions.

The author outside a healing church in NE Brazil

The Harvard anthropologist S.J.Tambiah, in his highly regarded studies into the interrelationship between Buddhism and spirit cults in North-East Thailand, documented the way in which Buddhist monks participate in a series of village rituals aimed at placating and warding off malign spirits and to support guardian spirits who may protect the wellbeing of the village (Tambiah, 1970). This would appear to have nothing to do with the Buddhist religion, with its core teaching on recognising and transcending suffering through human endeavour. However, the practices of the monks broadly represent a global phenomenon in which the major traditions of world religions have always adapted to and incorporated localised traditions in countries and regions they have spread to. In the process of this adaptation, indigenous rituals have often been revised to try to make them complementary to the dominant religion. Key religious professionals such as monks and priests may become central figures in administering these rituals. In doing so, the central teaching of the religion is not displaced but rather reemphasised through the use of traditional chanting and liturgies, but these are incorporated into ritualised contexts that may engage with belief systems that may be inconsistent with the central tenets of the religion. Arguably, the way religion manifests 'on the ground' is a product of a pragmatic accommodation with durable indigenous practices and beliefs in which coexistence and incorporation have been adopted. This may be a consequence of a failed attempt by force or persuasion to eradicate the local beliefs or a more benign desire to accept and respect indigenous traditions.

The example from Brazil is far from unique to that area and may be seen as sharing common ground with many traditional and folk practices of healing around the world. Sir James Frazer, writing in the 1920s, made the oft-cited and influential distinction between what he termed imitative and sympathetic magic. Sympathetic magic depends on the conviction that everything done to a certain object will in the same way affect the person to whom this object belongs or who is connected with it in any way. It is often associated with malevolent acts, whereby an effigy or a part of a persons' body is acted on in some way to cause misfortune (Frazer, 1990). However, the example cited from Brazil is one in which the creation of a representation of the body or mind is used to try to produce positive outcomes either for the petitioner or for the person they are concerned for. The priest's interpretation seeks to dismiss the idea that objects can be used to, in some way, bargain with the divine but are rather symbolic of a deep faith that is the real basis for successful healing.

Throughout the world, the relationship with particular places is seen as generative of healing. As we have noted, at a scientific level, there is now a strong body of evidence linking contact with the natural environment with improved mental health and wellbeing. By proxy, particular environments may also be seen as conducive to practices that are beneficial to wellbeing, for example, spiritual and religious centres for prayer and meditation. Retreat centres are routinely located in natural environments away from major transport intersections, population centres and intrusive technologies and mass media. There is a widely and implicitly held view that states of mental health are best nurtured in relatively calm and tranquil settings. These are also often places that prohibit or at least place restrictions on the use of digital technologies. As we have noted, throughout human history there has been a degree of consistency in viewing places that are close to nature and have a degree of detachment from commerce and industry as being conducive to wellbeing (Sternberg, 2011). The Victorians viewed living or at least spending time close to the sea as mentally and physically restorative while Japanese have lauded the benefits of warm mountain springs in natural settings for their healing properties.

Besides the benefits of their natural properties, places may have what can be called beneficial associative qualities arising from their histories. These are not so much as a consequence of some monumental historical event, such as the place of the martyrdom of St Thomas Becket or of the enlightenment of the Buddha, although it does not necessarily preclude these places. What I have in mind are places that may have some significance as locations where people may gather to contemplate, share ritual meals and enjoy sociable activities. They can be places where individual, family or community stories can be reflected on and future trajectories contemplated. Such places have particular significance for Native Americans as sites where the experiences of elders or ancestors can be reflected on as a way of learning lessons that may help steer wise paths in the future.

In his award-winning book *Wisdom Sits in Places*, Keith Basso writes of the significance of place to the Western Apache. At a simple level, places for the Apache may offer cautionary narratives, where such-and-such happened, for example, someone drowned in a creek at a particular crossing and in particular circumstances, and the stories from that place provide helpful warnings of dangers to be avoided. However, a deeper exploration of stories associated with places are seen as providing what to do and not to do in specific situations. Basso writes that, 'What typically happens is this. Something unusual occurs – an event or a series of events – that is judged to be similar or analogous to incidents described in one of the stories. Unless these similarities can be dismissed as superficial, they stimulate further thought, leading the thinker to treat the story as a possible aid for planning his or her own course of action. This is accompanied picturing in one's mind the exact location where the narrated events unfolded and imagining oneself as actually taking part in them, always in the role of a story character who is shown to be wise. If a powerful sense of identification with the character ensues ... the experience is taken to confirm that the narrative in question will be helpful in dealing with the situation in hand' (Basso, 1996, p.140). This deep, skilful contemplation of place and people is seen as leading to the development of a state of wisdom and mental health. The use of the imagination to participate in stories has been seen too within Ignatian spirituality, in which Gospel stories are entered into and experienced in a state of deep contemplation. There are parallels here too in Islamic traditions in which revered Islamic jurists use a process of 'reasoning by analogy' (*ijtihad*) to draw out lessons from traditional sources such as stories of the Prophet in the Hadith, to provide guidance on appropriate action in a contemporary situation (Codd, 1999). Place in these contexts can refer to imaginary settings evoked by landscapes or by scriptures and sacred narratives. The delving into a sea of stories to find guidance for action in the present is linked to many traditions from indigenous peoples in the Americas and Australasia to religious communities around the globe.

Implications for mental health and wellbeing focussed services

One immediate challenge is to consider the implications of the five ways to wellbeing for the development of services. These can provide an important tool in the design and evaluation of interventions. In considering research evidence presented above, one can see ways in which engagement with nature can enhance wellbeing. It can help people to connect both to others and to the natural environment. Nature can offer an important source for contemplation of change and interdependence and provide opportunities to learn about the natural environment. The philosopher Roger Scruton has argued that ecology will be enhanced if people see themselves as stewards of land and nature involving taking responsibility for it, and ensuring it is well maintained (Scruton, 2012). The responsible stewardship he envisages can be seen in the work of numerous conservation volunteers who maintain areas of natural beauty such as the West Highland Way in Scotland, the South Downs National Park in England and the national parks of North America. While there is a widespread acknowledgement that cleaning up the natural environment is a meritorious action, we are now witnessing a growing body of research that points to specific effects on mental health and wellbeing. The exhortation, in the five ways to wellbeing, to 'be active', 'connect' and 'keep learning' are responded to comprehensively by activities that engage people with nature. We are now seeing tangible initiatives that are bearing fruit in enhancing the mental health of participants – such as the Green and Open Spaces initiative in the South Downs National Park and the GROW project referred to above. Evaluations indicate these are among a growing number of examples of good practice that could be incorporated into mental health services (Shimmin et al., 2018; Adams and Morgan, 2016).

We have also noted distinctive challenges that may be faced by people from minority ethnic and cultural groups in feeling they have an entitlement to utilise natural resources. This is a challenge for those managing resources, for local GPs and other health and social care providers to ensure there is an agenda of inclusivity in representing and promoting use of these collective resources. Moreover, we have noted the considerable potential of horticultural- and other nature-based activities as a therapeutic practice for people who have experienced displacement, including loss of home and cultures. Engagement with the natural environment can in these contexts provide refugees and other migrant groups with a sense of belonging, of metaphorical and literal 'rootedness'. In practical terms this may point to the rolling out of therapeutic programmes such as offered by Freedom from Torture in the UK, or community food gardens in Australia. We have also noted the therapeutic benefits that may be derived from being in particular places, such as 'forest bathing' in Japan or locations associated with healing or community memories. These offer reflections for those designing and organising mental health services. Perhaps a cornerstone of practice can be engagement with people to determine *where* they feel good, what kind of environments enhance their wellbeing and to incorporate these perspectives into therapeutic programmes.

6 | Emerging Paradigms in Mental Health and Wellbeing Services

Chapter Overview

- There is compelling research evidence demonstrating the positive impact of mindfulness on certain mental health problems.

- Mindfulness-based cognitive therapy (MBCT) has been adapted from traditional Buddhist meditation techniques and has been incorporated into mainstream health services such as the National Health Service in the UK.

- There is ongoing debate on the merits of disengaging mindfulness practice from wider aspects of Buddhism where it is viewed as inextricably linked to ethical practice. Further debate concerns the extent to which it is an essentially solitary endeavour and implications for social support and sociability.

- The therapeutic potential of human interaction is demonstrated by the growing movement towards introducing Open Dialogue into mental health services. There is compelling evidence supporting this approach in addressing psychosis.

- Systemic Family Constellations offers an approach towards resolving ongoing problems in families through focussing on healing intergenerational conflicts. While it has been the subject of limited research, there is some evidence of beneficial effects in resolving relationship problems.

I recall offering a workshop presentation at a conference of the World Federation for Mental Health in Dublin in 1995. My presentation was on mindfulness and Buddhist meditation and was the only one of the subject of mindfulness at the conference. There were only a handful of people present and my sense was that the topic was considered rather marginal and esoteric. I was aware of mindfulness from studying Buddhism in the late 1970s and early 1980s, and from practicing meditation from 1977. At the time I held a lectureship in mental health at the University of Kent and was interested in exploring the potential interface between mindfulness meditation and mental health. The participants listened politely before going on to consider more pressing matters such as user involvement in services, treatment in the community, changing professional roles and the pace of deinstitutionalisation.

If one fast-forwards to 2018 there has been what can only be described as an explosion of interest in the topic of mindfulness. Approximately 500 academic papers on various aspects of mindfulness are being published every year. Prestigious universities regularly hold conferences and symposia on the subject and some, such as Oxford University, have started research centres. A major conference on the topic, one of many regular international events, was held in Amsterdam in the summer of 2018, attracting many of the major figures in the field. The conference themes testify to the breadth of the topic and its impact on the field of mental health and wellbeing. These included mindfulness in the workplace, mindfulness-based childbirth and parenting, mindfulness-based cognitive behaviour therapy, mindfulness for patients with stress-related somatic disorders, mindful management of organisations, online mindfulness, mindfulness in health professionals education, mindfulness and self-compassion and the neurocognitive mechanisms of meditation (program International Conference on Mindfulness (ICM), 2018 www.cmc-im.org). Contributions came from a wide range of disciplines, including clinical, neurological and developmental branches of psychology, medicine, organizational research and education, with the explicit aim of furthering our understanding on how mindfulness can contribute to wellbeing and relieve suffering. The level of interest in mindfulness is at least as strong across the Atlantic. An annual Mindfulness in America summit is hosted by one of America's best-known news anchors, Anderson Cooper, and draws together world-famous mindfulness teachers and speakers from the academic world, media, new technology, health professions, politics, education and even the US military. The summit website describes the aim of the event is no less than 'Through Talks, Interviews, Meditations, and Small Group Exercises, together we will explore how we can create a truly mindful society – in education, healthcare, politics, and more' www.mindfulnessinamericasummit.com (accessed 3rd September 2018). The focus is to show how mindfulness practice can be a route towards both individual and social transformation.

Mindfulness has an increasingly pervasive influence in the UK in the fields of mental health and wellbeing, education, criminal justice, work environments and most recently in the police and military. The Mindfulness Initiative was launched in 2013 growing out of a programme of mindfulness teaching for politicians in the UK Parliament. Its role is to 'investigate the benefits, limitations, opportunities and challenges in accessing or implementing mindfulness training and, based on these findings, educate leaders, service-commissioners and the general public'. The initiative has quickly gained momentum in the UK Parliament, with members of both the House of Commons and the House of Lords undertaking an eight-week Mindfulness Based Cognitive Therapy course. By January 2018, 165 British MPs and peers and 250 staff in the Houses of Parliament had taken the course. A parliamentary group – the 'Mindfulness All-Party Parliamentary Group – was formed in 2014 with the stated aim: 'To review research evidence, current best practice, extent and success of implementation, and potential developments in the application of mindfulness within a range of policy areas, and to develop policy recommendations for government based on these findings'. The Mindfulness Initiative supported the parliamentary group to undertake an inquiry into how mindfulness practice could be incorporated into UK services and institutions. The inquiry focussed in particular on five areas: education, healthcare, work, criminal justice and teaching standards (focussing on the potential accreditation of mindfulness teachers). The healthcare component was particularly oriented towards mental health and the potential impact of mindfulness on depression, tackling long-term mental health problems and improving prevention. The Group makes the following argument in favour of a mindfulness based approach citing an earlier government report on the merits of enhancing mental capital:

> The government's Foresight report developed the concept of mental capital, by which it meant the cognitive and emotional resources that ensured resilience in the face of stress, and the flexibility of mind and learning skills to adapt to a fast-changing employment market and longer working lives. It argued that developing the mental capital of the nation will be "crucial to our future prosperity and wellbeing". Qualitative research shows that mindfulness develops exactly these aspects of mental capital, encouraging a curious, responsive and creative engagement to experience. This should be of real interest to policymakers given the importance of improving productivity, and nurturing creativity and innovation in the UK economy. It is also an argument for why mindfulness has a role to play in the education system.

Source: Mindfulness All-Party Parliamentary Group, 2015

As noted above, mindfulness practice originated in, and is central to, Buddhism. At the core of the religion are the Four Noble Truths on the existence of suffering or unsatisfactoriness (*dukkha*), the cause of suffering, the end of suffering and the path leading to the end of suffering. A pivotal element of that path is mindfulness (*sati*), and it is, as such, a central aspect of the practice of Buddhism. The dramatic increase in interest and applications of mindfulness occurs at a time when Buddhism has continued to have a growing influence in many Western countries through the foundation of numerous monasteries of different Buddhist traditions in many countries including the UK, USA, Canada, Australia, New Zealand, Switzerland and Italy, and the widespread growth in lay Buddhist associations and meditation groups across the globe. This expansion has been accompanied by initiatives to apply Buddhism to various aspects of human wellbeing including the Zen Hospice Movement, the Zen Centre for Contemplative Care, Buddhist initiatives to support refugees and world peace and to act against climate change. While many meditation traditions of Buddhism have expanded in the West, in traditional Buddhist countries, the practice of meditation has often been neglected by lay people and even monastic orders. Richard Gombrich, founder of the Oxford Centre for Buddhist Studies, noted in fieldwork in Sri Lanka, that a relatively small percentage of Buddhist monks actually meditate and much practice is centred on study, ceremony and ritual (Gombrich, 1971). However, while this may be the case in terms of a general picture, Buddhist countries have generated highly influential meditation teachers whose impact has been considerable in the West.

Thus, at the time of writing, there are two powerful parallel movements, each with the practice of mindfulness at its core. Buddhism has regenerated in the West and well-reputed Buddhist teachers, both monks and laypeople, attract thousands of people to talks and retreats. Concurrently, what may be defined as secular mindfulness has, as noted, had an enormous and growing influence on many areas of public life. The renowned Buddhist scholar Stephen Batchelor observed, 'the practice of mindfulness, now widely adopted in health care, business, education, and other fields, has grown from a minority interest among dharma students into a global movement that draws people from all walks of life, most of whom have little interest in the traditional teachings or institutions of Buddhism (Bachelor, 2015, p.5). Indeed, given its firm roots and current place in Buddhist teaching and practice, it is perhaps surprising that there appears to have been an attempt to disconnect mindfulness practice from its ethical, cultural and religious origins. The question is of interest to intercultural enquiry and views differ as to the extent to which mindfulness can be simply extracted from the Buddhist context without losing some qualities of its practice. In Buddhism for example, for meditation practice to be fruitful, it is seen to be necessary to be accompanied by adherence to ethical principles. Through cultivating ethics the mind develops a level of peacefulness that is a necessary correlate of deepening meditation practice.

One of the foremost exponents of mindfulness practice in the West, Jon Kabat-Zinn, acknowledges that 'the systematic cultivation of mindfulness has been called the heart of Buddhist meditation'. However, writing in 1990, he argued that although mindfulness is most commonly taught and practiced within Buddhism, its essence is universal. 'It is a way of looking deeply into oneself in the spirit of self-enquiry and self-understanding. For this reason it can be learned and practiced ... without appealing to Oriental culture or Buddhist authority to enrich it or authenticate it ... In fact one of its major strengths is that it is not dependent on any belief system or ideology, so that its benefits are therefore accessible for anyone to test for himself or herself' (Kabat-Zinn, 1990, p.15). Interestingly, Kabat-Zinn's arguments for the merits of extracting mindfulness practice from Buddhism are not in some ways inconsistent with the approach to practice recommended by the Buddha himself. In a key Buddhist teaching the Buddha encourages his listeners not to believe in scripture, logic, parental tradition, common custom or even the words of a trusted teacher like himself, but rather to 'weigh the efficacy of any spiritual teaching or practice by the real wealth or goodness it brings to one's life' (Amaro, 2017a, p.399). However, while in essence Buddhism may be potentially accessible to a wide range of people, even the idea of following a religion may be off-putting to people who may otherwise find mindfulness practice beneficial. The goals of Buddhism – 'freedom from suffering' and the 'realisation of nirvana' – may be daunting to say the least, while focussing on modest goals such as learning to live more skilfully with chronic pain or reducing stress and anxiety may feel far more relevant and achievable.

Kabat-Zinn started his Stress Reduction Clinic at University of Massachusetts Medical School in 1979, integrating mindfulness and yoga into a programme aimed at helping patients suffering from chronic pain and stress. Doctors at the hospital could refer their patients to a course of eight weekly sessions in stress reduction and, in the first ten years of the programme some 4000 people were referred by more than 500 physicians. The basic course consisted of a 45-minute meditation session and patients were then expected to meditate daily for 45 minutes at home (Kabat-Zinn, 1990). The programme evolved into Mindfulness Based Stress Reduction, integrating various forms of meditation and relaxation and is at the present time the largest source of secular mindfulness training in the world (Michaelson, 2013). The approach has been accompanied by the development of the Mindfulness-Based Cognitive Therapy (MBCT) programme that is focussed on treating depression.

As Kabat-Zinn's programmes evolved, various research projects were undertaken to assess its impact on participants and more broadly on mindfulness-based interventions. Some of the benefits were:

- Cutting the relapse rate in half for people suffering from depression
- Lowering the rate of relapse of recovering addicts
- Improving attention, planning and organisational skills among school students
- Reducing ADHD symptoms in children
- Relieving anxiety and depression in people with social anxiety disorder
- Helping patients manage chronic pain
- Improving memory in older adults
- Countering age-related declines in brain function

The first of these benefits were identified by Teasdale and colleagues at the University of Cambridge. As a consequence of the rigorous methodology employed, this gave notice of the potential mental health benefits of mindfulness, and acted as something of a 'trail blazer' for subsequent studies (Teasdale et al., 2000). An examination of the content of Kabat-Zinn's programme reveals that it draws on a range of long-established Buddhist meditation and yoga techniques, including working with hatha yoga postures, body scanning, formal sitting meditation and bringing day-to-day mindfulness to everyday activities. Body scanning is a widely used meditation technique whereby sitting or lying down in silence attention is brought slowly and mindfully to each part of the body in a slow sweeping movement. Kabat-Zinn recommended to patients that they did this practice every day for 45 minutes in the first two weeks of the programme (1990, p.142). Additionally, patients were recommended to do mindfulness of breathing for 10 minutes of each day for the two weeks. In weeks three and four they were recommended to alternate the body scan with hatha yoga postures while increasing the mindfulness of breathing in the sitting posture for 15 to 20 minutes per day. Additionally, they were asked to pay particular attention to one pleasant experience per day in week three noting the physical, mental and emotional aspects of it as it was happening and to keep a calendar in which the experience was recorded. In week four the same attention was to be brought to the sensations and feelings associated with having an unpleasant experience. In weeks five and six patients were asked to increase meditation sittings to 45 minutes and could choose whether to focus on the breath, bodily sensations, sounds, feelings or on no particular object (Kabat-Zinn, 1990).

With the exception of using a calendar to record pleasant and unpleasant experiences, every component of the programme would be familiar to many people who had undertaken Buddhist mediation. Even the prescribed duration of sitting times to 45 minutes is consistent with that found in various well-established Buddhist traditions. As in Kabat-Zinn's programme, it is common practice in various Buddhist schools to start with the *anapanasati*, or 'mindfulness of the breath', and to move towards more generalised awareness. The practice of body scanning is a common one in many Buddhist schools, including the Thai Forest Tradition founded by the meditation master Ajahn Chah, and in the Burmese tradition as taught by the Buddhist lay teacher S.N. Goenka. The latter's meditation courses are offered in more than 130 mediation centres in over 94 countries of the world (Cassaniti, 2018, p.69). What is unique in Kabat-Zinn's programme is the way components from Buddhist traditions are integrated in an innovative way and made accessible to people from all walks of life. Through this, the programme has benefited people who would have never had the opportunity or perhaps inclination to learn about mindfulness practice. As Michaelson has remarked, individual stories of the impact of the programme on transforming people's ordinary lives are even more compelling than the growing weight of research evidence (Michaelson, 2013, p.21). One question however is whether it is necessary to play down or erase the Buddhist origins of the programme that are, as noted, integral to its central components. Would acknowledging this, while explaining how the components have been adapted in an innovative way, make the programme any less accessible and appropriate? Arguably to do so would be to recognise that the programme is genuinely intercultural in that it represents a meeting point and integration of different cultural traditions.

Some authors have expressed considerable scepticism about the merits of secularized mindfulness programmes, arguing that secular or what are often referred to as 'corporate' mindfulness serves as an instrument of consumer capitalism. Purser and Loy, for example, refer to the growth of 'McMindfulness', arguing that; 'Uncoupling mindfulness from its ethical and religious Buddhist context is understandable as an expedient move to make such training a viable product on the open market. But the rush to secularize and commodify mindfulness into a marketable technique may be leading to an unfortunate denaturing of this ancient practice, which was intended for far more than relieving a headache, reducing blood pressure, or helping executives become better focused and more productive' (Purser and Loy, 2013). Purser subsequently builds on this critique arguing that: 'Corporate mindfulness has become the new brand of capitalist spirituality, a disciplined but myopic self-help doctrine, that transfers the risk and responsibility for well-being onto the individual. As individuals are compelled to constantly self-monitor and self-regulate their internal states and "destructive emotions" by "being mindful," they become as Foucault warned "docile subjects." The formation of a neoliberal self is one that is autonomous and free to make rational choices that enhance human capital, bearing sole responsibility for its own welfare and happiness' (Purser, 2018, p.106).

Purser's critique is extensive and echoes wider criticism of governmental and corporate programmes aimed at enhancing populations' wellbeing. Besides producing the 'docile subjects' that Purser refers to, a wider critique of the 'happiness industry' is offered by Davies, who points to a convergence between therapeutic programmes and the widespread production of happiness-related science data that embeds society further into surveillance and micro-managerialist regimes of daily living. According to Davies, people are progressively being pulled away from subjective evaluations towards those supplied by technologies, and the economic agendas of others (Davies, 2015). One can think for example of the role of wellness and mindfulness apps in monitoring our exercise regimes and meditation sessions. Self-help books and programmes increasingly provide web-based resources and interactive technologies to ensure the participant follows the exercises fully and these in turn are directed towards a micro-management of daily life. Joanna Cook, an anthropologist, writing in the *Journal of Ethnographic Theory* argues that 'an analysis of political interest in mindfulness as "neoliberalism" frames subjectification as making people totally responsible for their mental health, detached from a broader socioeconomic and structural context' (Cook, 2016).

There are undoubted merits to these arguments and specific points about decoupling from the Buddhist tradition will be considered further below. Critical perspectives have been acknowledged in the report of the Mindfulness Initiative, that points to some shared scepticism, for example, among various stakeholders including trade unions (Mindfulness All-Party Parliamentary Group 2015). A concern is that mindfulness programmes may shift responsibilities for employees' wellbeing from company leaders and managers to the employees themselves. By being more mindful people may become more docile and put up with working conditions that they would otherwise complain about. The concern is that mindfulness may incline people towards passive acceptance in which, whatever conditions one is faced with, one should simply learn to accept them and get on with the job.

Such perspectives are perfectly understandable but stem from a misunderstanding of the essence of mindfulness practice. By being more 'in the moment' people become more, not less, attuned to the impact of the conditions around them. One can notice, for example, how a particular office environment affects mood, or responses when you have a particular interaction with a colleague. It can help in noting the effects of feeling overburdened by an excessive workload or of certain expectations on concentration and sense of wellbeing at work. A central component of mindfulness practice is the development of self-compassion that accompanies self-awareness. As awareness develops of the impact of conditions, steps can be taken to change aspects of the environment or behaviour, such as the layout of an office or being more careful in listening to a colleague. Mindfulness is therefore more appropriately seen as a foundation for skilful and compassionate *action* rather than a driver towards passivity. This distinction is recognised by the Mindfulness Initiative in pointing to the importance of also recognising the needs there may be for change in working environments, 'mindfulness has considerable potential across a very wide range of capacities needed in employment ranging from emotional resilience and empathy to cognitive skills and creativity. While it seems that mindfulness can offer real benefits for reducing stress and absenteeism, it is important to emphasise that as an isolated intervention it cannot fix dysfunctional organisations. Mindfulness will only realise its full potential when it is part of a well-designed organisational culture which takes employee wellbeing seriously' (Mindfulness All-Party Parliamentary Group 2015, p.77).

Paul Dolan, Professor of Behavioural Science at the London School of Economics, has expressed further concerns about the orientation of mindfulness programmes in promoting wellbeing. In his book, *Happiness by Design*, he argues that, 'Mindfulness definitely has its place. But I think it only goes so far for two reasons: first, people have to self-select into it; and second, it is quite effortful. The context-focused, rather than cognition-driven, approach ... only requires that you or someone close to you can influence your environment and, once that is done, it only then requires you to go with the grain of your human behaviour' (Dolan, 2014, p.153). Dolan orients his prescription for happiness on seeking pleasure through maximizing experience of things we enjoy or find worthwhile. These improve our mood and, by extension, those who enjoy good moods have a range of derivative benefits: 'There have been many studies to show, using causal methods, that those who experience better emotions live longer, are in better health, recover from viruses more quickly, take less time off work, are more successful in their careers, are generally more productive, and have happier marriages. In a study of siblings, kids who have a sunnier disposition are more likely to get a degree, get hired, and get promoted' (2014 p.82). The emphasis here is on generating positive emotions through doing things, such as associating with people whose company we enjoy, that improves our mood. A part of this is to tailor expectations that are reasonable and unlikely to engender disappointment.

Dolan reports evidence from a large-scale longitudinal study that shows that from childhood to adulthood, current income relative to previous income is a significant predictor of life satisfaction and mental health, whether people move up or down. He argues that modest expectations can help avoid 'false-hope syndrome whereby we stick with crazy expectations way past the point at which we should have reined them in' (Dolan, 2014 p.97 author's italics). This perspective resonates with findings from studies of migration. Links between expectation, disappointment and depression has been demonstrated in research into the wellbeing of refugees. Those arriving in a country that is a chosen destination often experience high expectations that can carry them through numerous challenges associated with being a refugee. Despite often experiencing arduous conditions, there are findings to suggest mental health problems are rarer than among those who have settled in a country and enjoy a reasonable level of security. At some point in the process, there is a realisation that expectations will not be met and the dreams that may have carried people across the globe will not be realities. It is in this difficult later period that refugees often experience depression (Beiser, 1999).

The difference in orientation between Dolan's prescription for happiness and that associated with mindfulness is important to reflect on. Dolan's view is that we should design our environment, based on the best research evidence, to generate the optimum conditions for happiness. Happiness, in turn, consists of feelings of pleasure and purpose and the generation of these feelings is ultimately, Dolan believes, all that matters. Mindfulness, by contrast, is orientated towards developing awareness, including awareness of feelings, thoughts and bodily sensations as they occur in the moment. The response to these is one of 'radical acceptance', in which feelings, even pleasurable ones, are not held on to but observed and understood as they arise and pass away (Brach, 2004, Ajahn Amaro, 2016). The aim is to develop comprehensive awareness of the moment rather than to generate a maximum amount of pleasurable feelings. Dolan's prescription may well work in designing the happiest possible life in terms of creating as many good feelings as possible but the human condition, according to the Buddhist teaching that inspired mindfulness practice, is (even in the best possible conditions), permeated by suffering in not getting what we want, in separation from the loved, in sickness and old age and so on. Mindfulness as such is arguably a practice that is generative of a mode of being that offers a durable inner peace in the face of lives vicissitudes.

Exercise 6.1

Example

The following advice on the practice of mindfulness is offered by the NHS, that incorporates comments by Professor Mark Williams from the Oxford Mindfulness Centre at Oxford University:

Becoming more aware of the present moment can help us enjoy the world around us more and understand ourselves better.

When we become more aware of the present moment, we begin to experience afresh things that we have been taking for granted.

Mindfulness also allows us to become more aware of the stream of thoughts and feelings that we experience and to see how we can become entangled in that stream in ways that are not helpful.

This lets us stand back from our thoughts and start to see their patterns. Gradually, we can train ourselves to notice when our thoughts are taking over and realise that thoughts are simply 'mental events' that do not have to control us.

Most of us have issues that we find hard to let go and mindfulness can help us deal with them more productively. We can ask: 'Is trying to solve this by brooding about it helpful, or am I just getting caught up in my thoughts?'

Awareness of this kind also helps us notice signs of stress or anxiety earlier and helps us deal with them better.

Exercise

Consider the opportunities and constraints there may be in introducing this approach into your workplace. What aspects of the workplace would have to be adapted to accommodate it, e.g. in terms of workplace routines, physical environment, etc.

Mark Williams and Danny Penman's book *Mindfulness: A Practical Guide to Finding Peace in a Frantic World* is perhaps a good example of this type of mindfulness publication that is widely available in railway stations, airports and shopping centres. The cover of the book describes it as a 'life-changing bestseller' and includes endorsements from Jon Kabat-Zinn and the American comedian and mindfulness practitioner Ruby Wax. Williams is the Founding Director and Honorary Senior Research Fellow at the Oxford Mindfulness Centre and was previously Professor of Clinical Psychology until his retirement, while Penman is a feature and comment writer for the *Daily Mail* and a mediation teacher. The combination of authors, with Williams' academic knowledge and rigour and Penman's lively prose style and experience of the subject matter, ensures this is an accessible and engaging book. It is accompanied by a 'free CD of guided meditations' and directs the reader to a wealth of secondary material including online resources. Consistent with observations of the 'secularisation' of mindfulness Williams and Penman do not even give Buddhism a cursory mention in the book, simply referring to mindfulness as 'a secret that was well understood in the ancient world and is kept alive in some cultures even today' (Williams and Penman, 2011, p.2).

Mindfulness is thus presented as though embedded in ancient esoteric knowledge that is now being unpacked and revealed to Western readers. The primary geographical origins of the practice in India and South East Asia is also obscured with reference to the 'ancient world' implying it may also be part of a common heritage practiced for example by the ancient Greeks. While there is some evidence of an equivalent to mindfulness practice being present in contemplative schools within other religious traditions (the Sufis in the Islamic tradition, Jainism, meditation schools in Hinduism and with some traces in Christian contemplative orders), the practice is foundational and most realised within Buddhism. The claim that it was a secret is also incorrect, as the Buddha spent some 40 years expounding the teaching to monks and laypeople and generations of meditation teachers have been open and inclusive in offering talks and retreats on the subject.

The apparent move to cut mindfulness off from its Buddhist roots may be of little immediate consequence to individuals who benefit from secularised versions of the practice. However, it may have longer-term implications for the development of mindfulness training. Given the continuing hub of expertise in the advanced practice of mindfulness that is available through Buddhist meditation traditions, the time may be ripe for enhanced dialogue between experts in secular and Buddhist approaches. This may be particularly beneficial for exploring ways to support those who have undertaken mindfulness based cognitive therapy or mindfulness based stress reduction programmes and want to deepen their practice. Interestingly, while reference to Buddhism may be absent in the central text, it is quite common for general books on mindfulness, including Williams and Penman's, to list resources at the back of the book that direct readers to Buddhist meditation centres, books and websites. These may constitute the only mention of Buddhism in popular books on the subject.

Williams and Penman trace the specific genealogy of their programme instead to Jon Kabat-Zinn's stress reduction programme and the mindfulness-based cognitive therapy programme developed by Williams, John Teasdale at the University of Cambridge and Zindel Segal at the University of Toronto. The Cambridge programme was designed for people who suffered repeated bouts of depression and was rigorously researched and evaluated by Teasdale and colleagues. As noted above, the results were impressive, demonstrating clinically that undertaking MBCT will halve the risk of depression in those who have suffered the most debilitating forms of the illness. Research evidence indicates that further benefits of MBCT include the following:

Decreases in anxiety, depression and irritability. Memory also improves, reaction times become faster and mental and physical stamina increases

Regular meditators enjoy better and more fulfilling relationships

Meditation has been found to be effective in reducing the key indicators of chronic stress, including hypertension

Also found to reduce the impact of serious conditions, such as chronic pain and cancer and can help to relieve drug and alcohol dependence.

Studies have shown that meditation bolsters the immune system and thus helps to fight off colds, flu and other diseases.

(Williams and Penman, 2011, p.6)

Mindfulness represents a compelling example of a practice that emerged in a specific religious and cultural context initially in India and spread across South East Asia before being embraced in the West. Arguably, the Western emphasis on mindfulness may be seen as something of a return to the core teaching of Buddhism. One prominent contemporary Buddhist practitioner, Ajahn Sumedho, an American monk and one of the earliest Westerners to be trained in the Thai Forest Tradition, describes mindfulness as the pivotal component of the Buddhist path. He distinguishes the secular practice of mindfulness with its focus on reliving stress, from the practice within the Buddhist monastic traditions where it is aimed towards realisation of the nature of human suffering and liberation from it. The successful practice of mindfulness meditation is, in this context, seen as inextricably linked to the adherence to moral precepts including not harming living beings, not stealing, refraining from harmful or exploitative sexual relations, being truthful and refraining from intoxicants. Being moral in this sense is seen as engendering peaceful states of mind that are conducive to meditation practice (Sumedho, 2014). The prominent scholar of Buddhism Richard Gombrich expresses his misgivings about meditation practice in the West partly on the grounds of a perceived absence of emphasis on ethics: 'I agree with the Buddha's teaching that sound ethics are a prerequisite for success in meditation; and sound ethics are based on unselfishness. Meditation in the West today, as I see it, is usually part of an essentially solitary pursuit of happiness. Learning to meditate on an (often misconceived) idea that one has no self is a self-centered activity that I think is likely to be self-defeating' (Gombrich, 2012).

The potential solitariness of meditation practice may also present a limitation to its effectiveness in enhancing wellbeing and mental health. As we have noted, there is now compelling evidence from social psychologists to support the view that participating in, and identifying with, social groups may be a vital component of wellbeing (see for example, Jetten et al., 2014). The anthropologist and mental health researcher Veida Skultans has pointed to the importance of collective memories or, more precisely, viewing personal memories as collective, in fostering a spirit of resilience. Writing on her native Latvia, she notes how Latvians, in giving accounts of adverse experiences during the Soviet occupation, often shift from an individual to a collective narrative, 'by switching from a singular to plural first person pronoun, from "I" to "we"'. This is not to discount the importance of personal memories but to 'embrace at one and the same time both the deeply personal and the intensely communal aspects of memory and identity' (Skultans, 2007 p.11). The perspective offered by Skultans is echoed in the social identity model of collective resilience offered by the social psychologist John Drury. Drawing on examination of the responses of people in London following the coordinated terrorist attacks in July 2005, Drury notes the positive role of the social dimension in generating resilience. He concludes that 'shared social identity based on group membership can explain social support and hence coping, survival and well-being even in the most extreme events' (Drury, 2012, p.210).

The view of mindfulness meditation as an essentially solitary endeavour is countered to some degree by pointing to the extent to which groups have been formed to support people in their practice. The Mindfulness Initiative itself has generated supportive socially based groups connected to schools, hospitals and workplaces. It may be argued that these support people to do a practice that is essentially solitary and one which can be done regardless of social support. A more fundamental challenge to the idea of mindfulness as solitary, isolated practice is offered by the Vietnamese Buddhist monk and peace activist Thich Nhat Hanh, who suggests using the concept of 'interbeing' to describe the relationship between the ostensibly subjective and objective perspectives on people and the world: 'Interbeing ... challenges us to look beyond the world of concepts and opposites. If we look deeply into the nature of our universe we can see all things as profoundly interdependent. At the heart of this understanding is the realisation that we have no separate self, that everything is empty of a separate self in a universe which is in a constant state of flux and change (Hahn, 1997)'.

Thus the practice itself engenders a sense of wellbeing that is fundamentally linked to a realisation of interrelationship and interdependence. Writing in the *Journal of Humanistic Psychology*, Dickson argues that Thich Nhat Hahn's concept of interbeing moreover challenges fixed views on the relationships between language and the world. The concept points to the interdependence and impermanence of phenomena and the suffering that is generated through seeking fixity in a world in flux. He draws parallels between Thich Nhat Hahn's concept of interbeing and the work of the influential German philosopher Gadamer (Dickman, 2016). For both, 'language itself is dependently emergent rather than being a discrete self-subsistent entity that we then attach to other dimensions of reality like a series of Post-It notes'. The emergence of language occurs in a dialogical context, in other words, in processes of interrelationship. Writing on Gadamer, the literary critic Terry Eagleton characterises his perspective as one in which 'all interpretation is situational, shaped and constrained by the historically relative criteria of a particular culture, there is no possibility of knowing a literary text "as it is"' (Eagleton, 2008, p.62). While Eagleton's reference point is literary texts, it is critical to understanding the wider insight Gadamer offers towards understanding dialogical processes, including those within therapeutic processes.

From the above arguments it is possible to discern some of the benefits, and potential limitations, of mindfulness. Its secularisation has been at the expense of disguising its Buddhist roots but it has adapted into programmes that are accessible to large sections of the populations in Western countries and many people are now benefitting from its practice who would probably have never encountered it. By introducing mindfulness as Buddhist it may have alienated people who were not religious or who have different religious backgrounds. The practice is, at the time of writing, being introduced into schools in England and it is quite possible that many would not have been happy to participate if it was seen as some imposition of ideas from an alien religion. On the other hand, the secularisation of mindfulness may be too sharp and may have divorced the practice from valuable and complementary orientations, such as its ethical base referred to above. The Buddhist precept to not kill living beings, for example, is foundational to generating a peaceful mind conducive to meditation. The employment of mindfulness practice by the US military offers a perspective divorced from this ethical basis. One challenge as mindfulness practices continue to grow in the West, is to support people who have incorporated it deeply into their lives and who could benefit from the guidance of those who are very accomplished in its application. There is merit in ensuring that practice in its secularised form is supported by also encouraging the development of meditation groups. There is also, as indicated above, potential benefits to be derived from generating forums for ongoing dialogue involving Buddhist teachers in the development of the practice.

The proposed scale of development of mindfulness based practices in the UK is significant, and testifies to the robust outcomes from research. The fact that it is endorsed by the National Institute for Clinical Excellence, the key institution for approving drug treatments and therapeutic interventions, is highly significant. Its application to the sphere of mental health in the UK is outlined as follows:

1. MBCT (Mindfulness-Based Cognitive Therapy) should be commissioned in the NHS in line with NICE guidelines so that it is available to the 580,000 adults each year who will be at risk of recurrent depression. As a first step, MBCT should be available to 15% of this group by 2020, a total of 87,000 each year. This should be conditional on standard outcome monitoring of the progress of those receiving help.
2. Funding should be made available through the Improving Access to Psychological Therapies training programme (IAPT) to train 100 MBCT teachers a year for the next five years to supply a total of 1,200 MBCT teachers in the NHS by 2020 in order to fulfil recommendation one.
3. Those living with both a long-term physical health condition and a history of recurrent depression should be given access to MBCT, especially those people who do not want to take antidepressant medication. This will require assessment of mental health needs within physical health care services, and appropriate referral pathways being in place.
4. NICE should review the evidence for Mindfulness-Based Interventions (MBIs) in the treatment of irritable bowel syndrome, cancer and chronic pain when revising their treatment guideline.

Source: Mindfulness All-Party Parliamentary Group, 2015

Open dialogue

The insights offered by Gadamer and by the Russian theorist Bakhtin underpin a major therapeutic initiative that emerged in the 1980s in Western Lapland and that has had considerable impact on the development of mental health services across Europe, particularly in Germany and Scandinavia. Open Dialogue is now recognised as an effective intervention for people suffering from psychosis and is, at the time of writing, part of a national pilot study within National Health Service in the UK. The NHS has justified its investment by pointing to impressive results from research into the approach: 'Some of the results so far from nonrandomised trials are striking. For example, 72 per cent of those with first episode psychosis treated via an Open Dialogue approach returned to work or study within two years, despite significantly lower rates of medication and hospitalisation compared to treatment as usual' (www.nelft.nhs.uk/aboutus-initiatives-opendialogue).

The international website on the Open Dialogue approach describes it as follows: The Open Dialogue approach is both a philosophical/theoretical approach to people experiencing a mental health crisis and their families/networks, and a system of care, developed in Western Lapland in Finland over the last 30 years or so. In the 1980s psychiatric services in Western Lapland were in a poor state, in fact they had one of the worst incidences of 'schizophrenia' in Europe. Now they have the best documented outcomes in the Western World. For example, around 75% of those experiencing psychosis have returned to work or study within 2 years and only around 20% are still taking antipsychotic medication at 2 year follow-up (www.open-dialogue.net).

The record of success of the Open Dialogue approach in Western Lapland is such that it has become a central, established part of the mental health system and has expanded beyond Finland to involve around 2,000 professionals. At its core, Open Dialogue draws on the insights of a range of philosophers, most notably Bakhtin, who stress the centrality of a dialogical approach in the analysis of literary texts. In Bakhtin's view language itself was to be seen as inherently 'dialogic' and grasped only in terms of its orientation towards another. To draw on Eagleton's concise account of Bakhtin's central ideas, societies should be seen as heterogeneous groupings composed of many conflicting interests and within them concepts are a focus of struggle and contradiction. 'Language, in short, was a field of ideological contention, not a monolithic system' (Eagleton, 2008, p.102).

When adapted to a therapeutic context, this insight has potentially far-reaching consequences. Besides philosophical influences found in Gadamer and, in particular, Bakhtin, the approach has therapeutic antecedents in the work of Bateson and in the Milan school of systemic family therapy. Bateson's theory of the double bind was particularly influential, in which a family member is faced with paradoxical contradictory injunctions, the following of either of which threatens withdrawl of parental love and support: 'The most useful way to phrase double bind description is not in terms of binder and a victim but in terms of people caught up in an ongoing system which produces conflicting definitions of the relationship and consequent subjective distress' (Bateson et al, 1962 cited in Seikkula and Olsen, 2003, p.405) The Italian team sought to counter this systemic problem by the technique of the counterparadox to untangle paradoxical communication. 'For instance, they would offer the family a new logic in the form of a positive connotation or a new ordering of behavior in the form of a ritual' (Seikkula and Olsen, 2003, p.405). However, the Milan approach, while offering an elegant theoretical model, was felt by the initiators of Open Dialogue not to work well in practice with the families they tried to support in Western Lapland. There was a sense of mutual discomfort in viewing the family as 'an object of therapeutic action, rather than as a partner in the therapeutic process' (ibid., p.406). From Seikkula and Olsen's writing on the genealogy of Open Dialogue, there is a clear sense that they were seeking an approach that did not constitute an imposition of a hitherto alien system on the Western Lapland location, but one that was sensitive to the organisational cultures of mental health in the region and the cultures of families and communities. In generating a good service fit for the communities they served, they drew on diverse therapeutic ideas and traditions and philosophical orientations to generate a suitable approach that was both effective and felt appropriate by the local populations.

A foundational figure in the development of Open Dialogue, the Finnish psychiatrist Jaakko Seikkula, articulated a fundamental distinction between monologic and dialogic language in the context of spoken language or utterance. David Trimble, a leading exponent of Seikkula's approach, describes it as follows: 'In dialogue, meaning is jointly produced in the space between speaker and listener. The developmental origins of individual mental life are found in exchanges of utterances between child and parent. The child develops the capacity to organize experience through internal reflective conversation, embodying both speaker and listener roles. Developmentally, dialogue is the original form; monologue emerges from its dialogical origins as a particular form of relationship between speaker and listener. In monologue, the listener is rendered passive; his or her sole function is to receive the utterances of the speaker' (Trimble, 2002, p.275). Trimble argues that, in therapeutic conversations, people have been wounded in some way and this wounding makes them understandably fearful of the inherent confusion and unpredictability of dialogue. They in turn seek safety in monologic constructions of themselves that offer a sense of order and certainty. These constructions are, however, delimiting and can cut the person off from listening to other voices that may offer new forms of action that can help address their predicaments. The monologic constructions moreover, impair the potential for social interactions: 'Their relationships become thin as they engage only with others who support their monologic positions, resisting those who contradict them and avoiding those who are open to seeing things in new and unexpected ways' (ibid., p.276).

Seikkula describes how over time there was a shift away from family therapy to open meetings with families informed by 'constructivist ideas, and then the idea of dialogism by Bakhtin, Voloshinov and Vygotsky' assisted in understanding the new phenomena. In the therapeutic process, neither patient nor family are seen as either the cause of the psychosis nor an object of treatment but 'as competent or potentially competent partners in the recovery process' (Seikkula and Olsen, 2003, p.405). The approach has three core features that are interdependent and recursive: tolerance of uncertainty, dialogism, and polyphony. Tolerance of uncertainty is generated through frequency of meetings in which the group learns to live with the ambiguities of the crisis situation. Seikkula describes situations when the group may meet every day for 10 to 12 days. This generates a space in which one can move from a monological perspective on the situation driven by perceived pressures on time to come up with 'the solution' to the problem. The question generated by the crisis 'what shall we do?' is held until the collective dialogue itself produces a response or dissolves the need for action. Dialogue occurs in the concrete, often mundane, particularities of human experience, in what Bakhtin (1984) called the 'once-occurring event of being'. Thus, as team members solicit the voices of all the participants in the meeting, they are constantly focused on what is taking place in the moment (Seikkula and Trimble, 2005). While the crisis has brought matters to a head in often disturbing ways, within a dialogical context it may also become an opportunity to make and remake the fabric of stories, identities, and relationships that construct the self and a social world (Seikkula and Olsen, 2003, p.409). The third feature, polyphony, is described in terms of the generation of multiple expressions, with no attempt to uncover a particular truth. It is contrasted to the systemic approach of the Milan group which sought to uncover the 'rules of the game' within families. The emphasis instead is on the generative power of open expression where utterances are allowed to take shape in dialogic spaces.

In terms of practical arrangements, the meetings bring together the person in acute distress with the team and all other important persons (ie., relatives, friends, and other professionals) connected to the situation. It takes place physically in an open forum, with everyone sitting in the same room, in a circle (Seikkula and Olsen, 2003, p.406). The atmosphere is one in which disparate voices are encouraged to be heard with respect and compassion. Those trained in the approach stress that their own attitudes are key contributory factors in the success of the sessions and set the tone for the other participants. A frequently used reference is to the importance of 'embodiment' to convey a sense of awareness of the moment to moment dynamics of the meeting. The atmosphere has to be one where participants feel safe to speak and 'enough security will be provided to proceed to the 'not-yet-spoken-experiences' (Seikkula, 2002, p.284). Trimble argues that the dialogic stance described by Seikkula has much in common with spiritual practice, 'as one relinquishes one's efforts to grasp and control the world, one can allow oneself to be held by a reality larger than oneself' (Trimble, 2002, p.276).

Aspects of the approach resonate with personal experience outside clinical contexts. I had a disagreement with an old friend in which we had very divergent views on a contemporary aspect of British society. It was an issue I had thought about and been preoccupied with in some of my academic writing for a long time and about which I had strong views. My friend took a diametrically opposite view that I felt was informed more by fashionable opinion than empirical research. We expressed our divergent views in person and then followed with a heated email exchange. I felt a sense of righteousness whenever I reflected on the exchanges and an overwhelming view that I was right. I became periodically detached from the people around me and regularly and repeatedly shared my point of view on the matter with family members. Mentally I amassed numerous examples to show that I was right and he was wrong. I felt tense as the time got closer to our next meeting but also very well-equipped to soundly beat him in any argument on the topic. Around this time I read a little book by a meditation teacher that focussed on human interaction with the stark title *I'm Right and You're Wrong*. The book offered reflection on the role of fixed views and how grasping at proving you are right and the other person is wrong can shut down potential for growth in relationships. Instead, the book encouraged an attitude of developing awareness towards the holding of fixed views, awareness of the mental and emotional states that arise with the views and the effect on the body when they arise. It also encouraged being with the other person in an attentive and 'present' way and not trying to 'win' anything (Amaro, 2016).

This orientation is consistent with Trimble's description of the dialogical approach, of relinquishing efforts to grasp and control the world. In the therapeutic encounter, family members and close friends are likely to arrive with some fixed views about the cause of the crisis and the actions that must be taken to resolve it. These are likely to oppose or contradict the views of other members of the group and an orientation towards 'winning' and proving you are right and they are wrong is likely to open further conflict. Instead, in the Open Dialogue approach the utterances are held in the group and the dialogical movement towards understanding often gives rise to completely new perspectives on the crisis. In the case of my subsequent encounter with my friend, rather than try to win the argument by mustering the evidence to support our views, we instead talked about the process itself and the impact it had on us emotionally. Our difference of view remained unresolved while the meeting gave rise to the development of an even deeper friendship, in which the matter that had preoccupied us diminished in importance.

Reflections on shamanism and family constellations

The therapeutic potential of engaging with a 'reality larger than oneself' may be seen to underpin many healing systems. The psychiatrist and anthropologist Arthur Kleinman refers to processes of symbolic healing as involving the presence of a 'symbolic bridge' between personal experiences, social relations and cultural meanings (Kleinman, 1988, p.131). He argues that healing, whether sacred or secular, achieves its efficacy through the transformation of experience and that this is accomplished through culturally authorised interpretations. He provides a range of examples, including that of a Taiwanese shaman who offers dramatic reinterpretation of afflictions, introducing a 'master myth' in which a reassuring, effective spirit dominates his consciousness and transforms his condition. In describing the work of a shaman in a celebrated (if sometimes contested, see Taussig, 1987) essay, Levi-Strauss refers to a transition that will be made 'from the most prosaic reality to myth, from the physical universe to the physiological universe, from the external world to the internal body'. The work of the shaman involves a ritual in which there is 'rapid oscillation between mythical and physiological themes, as if to abolish in the mind of the sick woman the distinction which separates them, and to make it impossible to differentiate their respective attributes' (Levi-Strauss, 1979, p.193). In these accounts, shamanism is described in terms of reinterpretation of realities, movement from, say, an individualised affliction to one understood in mythological or cosmic terms. The shaman works to understand and reorder an unseen world through visualisation and ritual. In doing so s/he provides an explanatory model culturally understandable to the afflicted and to her or his community.

It is arguable, however, that processes of symbolic healing do not necessarily involve building bridges between personal experiences and culturally authorised interpretations. People may experience healing through engaging with processes that were hitherto unknown and esoteric and grapple with explanatory models that introduce unfamiliar concepts and explanations for their conditions. An example may be the contemporary practice of family constellations developed by Hellinger, a former Catholic missionary who left the priesthood and forged a career as a therapist. Hellinger's approach is another example of an intercultural orientation in that has involved transitions from diverse cultural contexts and transformation into a new system that has been incorporated as a healing modality particularly in Europe and Latin America, with several hundred practitioners in the UK. Hellinger developed his theories and models of practice while working in South Africa and observing traditional rituals among the Zulu. He lived there for 16 years, became fluent in the Zulu language, participated in their rituals, and gained an appreciation for 'their distinct worldview' (Cohen, 2006). His evolving philosophy and therapeutic methods were particularly influenced by phenomenology, Zulu ancestor reverence and family systems therapy. In turn, his phenomenological approach was influenced by by a range of influential philosophers and theorists, including Bretano, Husserl and Heidegger. In terms of the Zulu influence, he was impressed by what he saw as the dignity of the relationship to parents and to ancestors: 'The ancestors are regarded as positive, constructive, and creative presences. Failure to show them proper respect invites misfortune; proper veneration ensures benefit' (Cohen, 2006, p.228).

The goal of a family constellation, in particular, is to help the client gain insights into, understand, and, finally, change, his or her inner image of a conflictive experience within the family system, for example, a dysfunctional relationship with a partner or parent(s). This is typically administered in a group setting in which approximately 25 unrelated participants meet for a one-time, three-day, facilitator-led intervention called a "family constellation seminar" (FCS). FCSs do not work with whole families, and they are not multi-family groups. They can be considered an individual-focused, short-term group therapy intervention. They do not represent a comprehensive treatment program (Hunger et al., 2014).

While Hunger and colleagues are correct to point to the short-term focus of individual seminars, those who participate in seminars are often involved in long-term processes of training and mentorship, sometimes lasting several years. The methods used may be seen as having some parallels to Open Dialogue and are also influenced by phenomenology and systemic family therapy. However, in many respects, family constellation lies firmly outside mainstream mental health care. Its influences from shamanism and traditional indigenous healing systems, including ancestor reverence, are unlikely to enhance claims to credibility within mainstream mental health professions. There have been concerns too with respect to attitudes towards abuse within family groups and perceived enforcing of patriarchal structures. The approach has a strong emphasis on inclusivity, even for family members who may have behaved badly, within a multigenerational family system that includes children, their parents and grandparents, the parents' siblings, and sometimes great-grandparents. Every member is seen as having a special place, including a previous spouse, a deceased child or a stillborn baby. Deceased members of the family are included so long as a current family member has a significant memory of that person (Stiefel et al., 2002).

The integration of members of the family system is through realising bonds of love and, according to the model, it is important that no one is excluded even as noted, if they have behaved in reprehensible ways. In the therapeutic process ownership of offensive or disruptive actions becomes less oriented towards blaming a particular individual, than held in the context of an interdependent family group. According to Stiefel, a psychologist, and Harris, a psychotherapist, 'Hellinger assumes that extended family groups have a group conscience. The group conscience is governed by principles of fairness and loyalty. The rules of the conscience bind family members to the group in the form of "moral" obligations. The group conscience acts in the service of the group but the processes remain largely outside people's conscious awareness' (Stiefel et al., 2002, p.40). The anthropologist Whitney Duncan notes an emphasis within the practice of systemic family constellations on tapping into a power or energy that lies outside individual consciousness: 'In an important sense, all subjectivity ... is understood and interpreted as a particular form of intersubjectivity, one explicitly predicated on the "porousness of the self" to the Other' (Duncan, 2017, p.499).

The idea of group consciousness in this context is informed by the work of the scientist Rupert Sheldrake, who introduced the concept of morphic fields as organising principles for natural phenomena. Sheldrake argues that, besides organising nature, morphic fields have memories and subtle modes of communication that transcend constraints of time and space. He provides as examples the movement of flocks of starlings or shoals of fish as indicating how this system works in nature. He argues that humans have comparable families of morphic fields that link generation to generation. Sheldrake agrees with Hellinger that the exclusion of a member or members of a family can have repercussions across generations and create unresolved tensions and conflicts (Sheldrake et al., 2000; Mayer and Viviers, 2016). Within the context of the practice of systemic family constellations, people are invited to act out roles in which they assume the positions of key people in the family group, including the ones who have been excluded. In the seminars, the person representing the excluded family members is symbolically invited back into the family unit and this is experienced by participants as a source of familial healing.

While Open Dialogue has been the subject of nonrandomised control trials and clinical follow-up studies, and these have formed a basis for justifying incorporation of the approach into mainstream mental health services, there has been little such work on family constellations. This may be partly due the lack of a psychometrically sound instruments to evaluate the approach, as Hunger and colleagues suggest, but it may also be a consequence of the nature of the approach itself. Open Dialogue has emerged through addressing the cultural limitations of a systemic family approach derived from metropolitan Italy to communities in Western Lapland. The cultural transition that took place incorporated an egalitarian approach towards the mode of working with families that engaged with them as partners in therapeutic processes in which they co-interpreted the crisis situation and worked towards its resolution. Therapists, as such, did not stand outside the process interpreting hidden 'rules of the game' –as in the Milan approach – but felt their way forward with family members in a relatively egalitarian way.

In the case of systemic family constellations, the process is arguably less equal in that an experienced facilitator moves the process forward. It is also based on explicit metaphysical orientations that may appear esoteric to the general population and therefore likely to involve people who are more generally oriented towards what are often described as 'new age' philosophies. Seminars are often offered in festivals that include an array of therapeutic modalities that sit outside mainstream health and social care. Moreover, the approach is not specifically oriented towards people in crisis or, indeed, with mental health problems. Interventions are aimed towards experiencing healing of unresolved problems and provide opportunities for people with similar outlooks to share deeply personal experiences together in an atmosphere of mutual understanding. Despite the relatively select group who use the approach, there is however some emerging evidence that its outcomes are sufficiently beneficial that it could form an effective therapeutic modality in social care settings.

One promising piece of research is a randomised control trial (RCT) undertaken by a research group at Heidelberg University Hospital. The group did an in-depth examination of the organisation of family constellation seminars and developed a standardised format. Methodologically, they introduced a new psychometric rating scale to reflect dimensions consistent with those that facilitators were seeking to achieve in these sessions, including measurements associated with belonging, autonomy, accord and confidence. The study was undertaken in accordance with the rigour required of an RCT. The researchers concluded that: 'Our findings suggest that FCSs (Family Constellation

Seminars) have positive effects on the experience in personal social systems in an adult population presenting with relationship problems, particularly conflictive experience within their families' (Hunger, 2014 p.301).

In sum, the approaches identified above point to significant ways in which the landscape of mental health and wellbeing services is being transformed. The initiatives described are examples too of what I characterise as an interculturalisation of mental health and wellbeing. They display the movement of ideas and practices within the context of an unprecedented levels of human migration. Mindfulness practice is an example of both transitions and transformation. As we have noted, its origins in the West spring from colonialism, the movement of populations from Buddhist countries to resettle in North America and Europe and the travels to South East Asia of seekers from the West, notably from the 1960s onwards. From experiencing the practices of Buddhist meditation, key figures such as Jon Kabat-Zinn have transformed core elements into programmes so that they can be incorporated into the structures of Western healthcare. We have noted that the secularised approach to mindfulness has offered therapeutic opportunities to people who would probably never seek instruction in a Buddhist *vihara* or Buddhist meditation group. It is also integrated into therapeutic programmes that have been the subject of extensive scrutiny and evaluation, including RCTs. While there has been significant research on the links between mindfulness, and meditation practices more generally, brain chemistry understanding of associated physiological and psychological processes are at an early stage. What is clear is that mindfulness practices have significant, discernible, positive impacts on mental health and wellbeing. This underpins recognition by the National Institute for Clinical Excellence in the UK, its incorporation into the NHS, and the rolling out of its practice into schools and workplaces as recommended by the Parliamentary group.

As noted above, Open Dialogue is also gaining traction as an accepted therapeutic intervention. There is little understanding of the precise processes that make it successful but its development has been underpinned by robust research evidence of its effectiveness in Finland including a two-year follow-up on first episode schizophrenia (Seikkula et al., 2003) leading to further studies in the UK. Another important feature of mindfulness based approaches and Open Dialogue is that they have been shown to be effective for people suffering from discernible mental health problems and as such address a core requirement of mental health services.

Mindfulness is recommended by the National Institute for Health and Care Excellence (NICE) as a way to prevent depression in people who have had three or more bouts of depression in the past.

Source: NHS www.nhs.uk/conditions/stress-anxiety-depression/mindfulness/ (accessed 31st August 2018).

7 | Conclusion: Towards an Integrated, Intercultural Approach in Mental Health and Wellbeing

A central argument here is that our understandings of mental health and wellbeing are increasingly informed by dynamic intercultural contexts. The pace of change in the field is accelerating in an unprecedented age of migration in which people from a wide diversity of cultural and religious traditions are interacting with each other in growing and diversifying urban and rural spaces. People are also interconnecting with one another in new ways through the growth of digital technologies that are offering resources for promoting and sharing understandings and representations of what constitutes living well. These resources often arrive involuntarily through advertising. A news programme may be interspersed with advertisements for drugs, diets or aids to exercise regimes aimed at enhancing wellbeing. Newspapers, whether in print or digital form, routinely carry supplements with titles such as 'Wellbeing', 'Living Well' or, in the case of the *New York Times*, 'Smarter Living'. These supply a heterogeneous range of lifestyle and health guides that are informed by highly diverse and intercultural understandings of mental health and wellbeing. One discernible and significant trend is towards more holistic understandings of mental health that recognise a dynamic interaction between mind, body, social and material environments and, in some traditions 'soul' or spirit'. In this sense, how we think about mental health may be seen as informed increasingly by a wellbeing paradigm that is being shaped by intercultural perspectives.

Current research is revealing a dynamic interaction between physical and mental health manifest for example in number of recent studies demonstrating the positive impact of exercise regimes on depressive symptoms. In a controlled study of 22,000 Norwegian adults over an 11-year period, it was found that those who exercised were less likely to develop depression, with even as little as one hour of exercise per week proving beneficial (Harvey et al., 2017). Researchers from the University of Limerick, writing in the *Journal of the American Medical Association*, have identified strong links between exercise regimes and the reduction of symptoms associated with depression such as low mood and feelings of worthlessness.

Specifically, people who do resistance exercises like weight lifting and strength training may experience fewer depression symptoms (Gordon et al., 2018). Other studies have pointed to the benefits that physical exercise holds for older adults. Lautenschlager and colleagues from the University of Western Australia assessed the impact of physical activity on cognitive impairment and depression in later life and conclude that, 'It can be seen that physical activity, like a number of other lifestyle interventions, holds the promise of better mental health outcomes for older adults. Such an intervention has the advantage of being safe and inexpensive and produces a wide range of health benefits' (Lautenschlager et al., 2004).

While much more needs to be learned about the mechanisms whereby physical processes may enhance or undermine mental wellbeing, what is clear is that there is increasing awareness of the dynamic interactions of mind, body and society as demonstrated by a biopsychosocial orientation to mental health. Far from the dualism between mind and body proposed by Descartes, we are now recognising not only the vital interrelationships between mind and body but also encompassing environment, in the form of both the natural and social worlds. This interrelationship is acknowledged and underpins common frameworks for understanding and assessing wellbeing as for example in the wellbeing triangle that highlights the interplay between material, social and subjective wellbeing (White, & Abeyasekera, 2014).

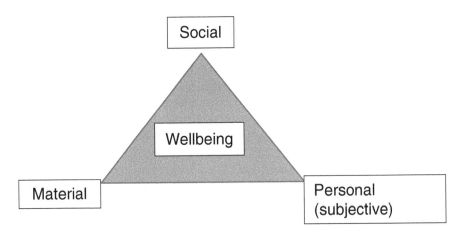

Figure 7.1 Wellness Triangle

There is a discernible *orientation towards integration* to be found in both emerging paradigms in research and in the configurations of mental health services. Just as evidence of the interplay between mind and body is noted above so to, in for example the results of extensive research collaborations by Jules Pretty and others, we note compelling evidence of how both mind and body are affected by the environment. Green Exercise exemplifies this paradigm shift in developing and incorporating wellbeing regimes that act simultaneously on mind, body and environment (Pretty, 2005). A major challenge for the 21st century is to incorporate these new paradigms in service configurations that are structured to reflect the interaction of domains of body, mind and society through transformation of salient disciplines such as psychology, psychiatry, psychotherapy, physiological medicine and social work.

There is evidence that this significant challenge is beginning to be addressed through initiatives that may open doors to the provision of services that encompass mind, body and environment. Even the idea of prescribing, once inexorably associated with the prescription of medicines occasioning a trip say from the GP surgery to the pharmacist, is now being increasingly seen in holistic terms. A number of health, mental health and economic benefits have been identified with the introduction of 'social prescribing' that links patients in primary care and their carers with non-medical sources of support within the community. According to The King's Fund, an influential charity that aims to improve health care in England, social prescribing may be defined as 'a means of enabling GPs, nurses and other primary care professionals to refer people to a range of local, non-clinical services. Recognising that people's health is determined primarily by a range of social, economic and environmental factors, social prescribing seeks to address people's needs in a holistic way. It also aims to support individuals to take greater control of their own health. Social prescribing schemes can involve a variety of activities which are typically provided by voluntary and community sector organisations. Examples include volunteering, arts activities, group learning, gardening, befriending, cookery, healthy eating advice and a range of sports' (www.kingsfund.org.uk/publications/social-prescribing).

The authors of an evaluation study of social prescribing conclude that, 'It is tailor-made for voluntary and community led interventions and can result in:

- better social and clinical outcomes for people with long-term conditions and their carers
- more cost efficient and effective use of NHS and social care resources
- a wider, more diverse and responsive local provider base'. (Dayson and Bashir, 2014, p.4)

The authors go on to note that, 'patients and their carers have experienced improved mental health, become more independent, less isolated, more physically active, and begun engaging with and participating in their local community. They have also been able to access a range of welfare benefits that they were previously unaware of' (ibid., p.4).

At the time of writing, the NHS in the UK is undertaking a national consultation on social prescribing and influential public sector bodies such as the National Institute for Clinical Excellence, NHS England and the College of Medicine are at the forefront of investigating ways in which social prescribing can be integrated into the mainstream of one of the worlds major healthcare systems. Dr Michael Dixon, a GP and co-chair of the College of Medicine described the approach as follows: 'In a practice like mine, somebody, a link worker, who is not medical, takes aside a patient and finds out what their hopes, beliefs, challenges and obstructions are. They then offer them a whole range of possibilities, which, for someone who's depressed, might vary from walks and talks to looking at things online to social groups to maybe going to an educational session on healthy breathing, self-hypnosis, or whatever, but not immediately reaching for the tablet' (College of Medicine, 2018). Social prescribing offers the potential for radical rethinking of the relationship between patient and doctor in which referral exceeds the bounds of what is conventionally thought of as 'medical' intervention. As one social prescribing advocate put it, 'we are concerned more with what matters to patients than what is the matter with patients' (ibid, 2018). Those supporting social prescribing envisage GPs having the potential to refer or direct patients to wide array of interventions and practices either directly or through a 'link worker'.

Moreover, medical schools in the UK are increasingly engaged with training that incorporates social prescribing. The College of Medicine noted that 'new outcomes for graduates published by the General Medical Council (GMC) emphasise the need to apply social science principles as well as health promotion, patient empowerment, and shared decision-making. As the gap in teaching is being filled and most medical schools are embracing the biopsychosocial model, it is key to ensure high quality teaching for the next generation of clinicians and healthcare professionals' (Chiva Giurca, 2018).

The introduction of social prescribing opens the door to the incorporation of a wide range of interventions, with diverse cultural roots, into mainstream health and social care. Practices such as mindfulness, tai-chi and yoga are already recognised as potentially beneficial for a range of health conditions with tai-chi and yoga being available through referral from physiotherapy services in some NHS trusts. Mindfulness, as noted, is already recommended by a range of NHS and GP practices. As such, social prescribing offers a challenge to analytical models of healthcare that differentiates between mainstream professionalised services, 'folk' or alternative sectors and, following Kleinman, a popular sector that includes non-professionalised ideas and practices associated with health and wellbeing within communities (Kleinman, 1980). Instead social prescribing opens the possibility of a fully integrated system in which GP practices act as a hub drawing together diverse healing traditions.

While acknowledging that social prescribing has considerable traction, it is also important to recognise the significant challenges it faces before it can be fully incorporated into healthcare systems. The first of these may be identified as systemic. For example, in a context of insurance-based healthcare systems, there may be significant constraints on the range of services a GP may incorporate into a treatment plan without the patient incurring additional costs. Acupuncture, tai-chi, yoga and mindfulness-based practices may not be included as reimbursable expenses so would involve costs beyond that already met through the charges incurred through insurance cover. However, it should be noted that this is not necessarily the case and, in the USA for example, some insurance companies do support a range of alternative therapies. Moreover, this is not only a potential problem in relation to insurance-based systems. Most of these treatment modalities (with the exception of mindfulness-based therapies) are not available on the NHS or, if they are, only in limited forms and localities. What is both distinctive and challenging within the NHS context is the potential for the development of integrated programmes of care that do draw together perspectives and insights from a spectrum of treatment modalities.

A second challenge relates to professional attitudes and practices. There is considerable diversity of views found among GPs on the merits of treatments and interventions that fall outside a medical model and not all are convinced of the merits of social prescribing. Drawing on a study undertaken by the University of Manchester, some GPs have questioned the evidence base behind social prescribing. The study consisting of a systematic review of 15 studies of social prescribing in the UK concluded that, 'Social prescribing is being widely advocated and implemented but current evidence fails to provide sufficient detail to judge either success or value for money. If social prescribing is to realise its potential, future evaluations must be comparative by design and consider when, by whom, for whom, how well and at what cost' (Bickerdike et al., 2017).

Moreover, the introduction of training relating specifically to social prescribing is at an early stage and is, by no means, common in medical schools. While a specific focus on the implementation of social prescribing may be relatively uncommon, there is a general broadening of curricula to incorporate more social sciences and integrated approaches such as the biopsychosocial model. In the field of mental health there is increasing interest and engagement with more holistic and integrative approaches across a spectrum of disciplines and professions including social work, psychiatry, psychology, psychotherapy and mental health nursing (Kreitzer, 2015, Norcross and Goldfried, 2005). Moreover, prominent figures in the mental health field strongly advocate an integrated approach. In addressing the question of optimal care for people with long-term mental and physical health conditions, Graham Thornicroft and colleagues have emphasised the provision of integrated, holistic, and person-centred care. They identify an integrated approach as having three levels: 'The key issues at the macro level include the integration of activities at the policy or population levels, such as policy formation, budgetary allocation, and purchasing or payment. At the meso level, changes would occur within district, community, or primary care facilities, which would alter the care pathway for people with long-term conditions. At the micro level, services include targeting, goal setting, and planning, in which patients and providers focus on a specific problem and together set realistic and measurable goals, and develop an action plan for attaining those goals in the context of patient preferences and readiness' (Thornicroft et al., 2018 p.177).

The vision here for integrated mental health care is one in which service provider and patient work together in conceptualising and planning a programme that harnesses a range of community and healthcare resources. There are clear parallels with the core ideas behind social prescribing, although in social prescribing the mechanism for integration is more clearly conceptualised. The approach has been elaborated by the NHS in England, setting out an ambitious programme of interlinked initiatives that provide a context in which social prescribing could flourish (NHS England, 2019). GPs have been encouraged to participate in the scheme not least because of the potential for saving their time in working with patients who have needs outside the parameters of mainstream medical support. The Royal College of General Practitioners points out that GP workloads have been recorded as increasing by 16% between 2007 and 2014 owing to factors such as 'an ageing population with increasing incidence of multi-morbidity, a rising administrative burden from regulatory and statutory pressures, and inadequate resources'. In this respect social prescribing is identified as one of ten 'high impact actions' – a 'range of initiatives that were introduced with the aim of increasing capacity in general practice and reducing GP workload' (Royal College of General Practitioners, 2017). In a survey of 823 GPs in England commissioned by the Royal College of General Practice 31% reported introducing social prescribing to help reduce workload (ibid., p.7). There were however reservations expressed by GPs with respect to the implementation of the approach including the problems of keeping up to date with the diverse range of community facilities.

The model proposed by NHS England is ambitious and envisions a high degree of cooperation in terms of knowledge sharing and practical support across agencies. A social prescribing link worker sits at the hub of these disparate activities and has a role in building knowledge of local activities. The approach is similar to what I have previously referred to as 'micro level advocacy' in which a care worker builds knowledge of local resources she or he can integrate and mobilise in response to clients' diverse needs (Watters, 2008). A challenge in the social prescribing model is that the tasks involved are almost limitless and the relatively low-paid link workers (the report refers to a possible salary of £25,000) may find themselves dealing with unrealistic expectations. To counter this, NHS England has sought to define the parameters of the link worker role: 'Link workers typically work with people over 6 – 12 contacts (including phone calls and meetings) over a three-month period (depending on what the person needs) with a typical annual caseload of up to 250 people, depending on the complexity of people's needs and the maturity of the social prescribing scheme' (NHS England, 2019, p.18).

Figure 7.2 Social Prescribing Model
Source: NHS England (2019)

The model does offer the potential for harnessing and integrating a range of interventions and initiatives. For example, exercise and contact with nature, two of the 'ways to wellbeing' referred to earlier, could be offered through participation in a walking group that utilises a national park. A local tai-chi or yoga group could be commissioned to offer sessions aimed at enhancing physical and mental wellbeing, sessions in a mindfulness group may be offered to people suffering from depression, anxiety disorders and other stress related conditions.

An integrative approach also opens potential for engaging with arts and cultural activities. In the UK a parliamentary group was established in 2014 to 'improve awareness of the benefits that the arts can bring to health and wellbeing, and to stimulate progress towards making these benefits a reality all across the country'. The group conducted an enquiry over two years that drew on the perspectives of influential political figures and leading policy makers and practitioners in the arts, health and wellbeing. The 2017 report of the group entitled Creative Health: the Arts for Health and Wellbeing emphasised the potential for models of social prescribing to integrate arts-based activities (All Party Parliamentary Group 2017). Many of the activities described in the parliamentary groups report drew on initiatives that could be described as intercultural in terms of the origins of the activities, in how they engaged with diverse cultural and ethnic groups, and in leadership from researchers and practitioners from a range of backgrounds. In citing research evidence on the benefits of arts based activities, the group pointed to 'similarities between mindfulness and the "flow" that is typical of arts engagement – both require presence in the moment and a sense of absorption' (ibid., p.40). While offering an extensive range of examples of research projects that highlighted the benefits of arts based approaches, the group did point to the challenges of researching the arts as compared to 'relatively clear-cut nature of mindfulness', as against, 'the complexity and diversity of arts and health work has served as a disincentive to research funders' (p.40).

Exercise 7.1

Example

An Arts and Humanities Research Council-funded research project (2014–17) led by Professor Helen Chatterjee at University College London is investigating the potential of museums on prescription as part of the wider social prescribing landscape for older adults. Building on previous work with older adults, ten weekly two-hour programmes are being offered to vulnerable or lonely older adults (65–94) across seven museums in central London and Kent. The sessions combine activities such as gallery talks and tours, discussions, museum object handling and collections-inspired creative activities. The research involves exploration of the value of cultural heritage in overcoming social isolation and of the relationship between touch and wellbeing mediated by cultural artefacts. A range of qualitative analyses and quantitative scales is being used, including measurement of wellbeing and loneliness. Interim findings show a progressive increase in psychological wellbeing across sessions and some upward trend in social inclusion.

Exercise

Consider an arts facility or activity within your own locality. What arrangement could be made for people with mental health problems to engage with it? What are the likely outcomes?

Evidence was also offered on the importance of place to wellbeing and mental health and how some designs enhance healing. Sunand Prasad, former president of the Royal Institute of British Architects (RIBA), has said that: 'The environment of the arts and beauty and spirituality can all be part and parcel of recovery, whether it be from physical or mental conditions' (p.66). The group considered evidence of the merits of a range of architectural initiatives, including ways that nature could be integrated more closely into the design of hospitals and centres for continuing care. The report of the Parliamentary Group acknowledges the strong interrelationship between engagement with the natural environment and enhanced wellbeing. It references the report Wellbeing and Policy in which Lord Layard, a leading academic expert on wellbeing and co-authors recognise that 'physical or visual access to green spaces, water, or natural light appears to have a surprisingly powerful direct impact on subjective wellbeing' (p.64). While some may be perplexed that leading experts find the relationship between exposure to nature and wellbeing 'surprising', it is perhaps more important that these linkages are recognised by such influential figures in the field. Moreover, it is notable that the influences of environment on subjective wellbeing and mental health is recognised and underpins the development of building programmes in which healing is perceived in terms of the effects of interrelationships between humans and the built environment.

What the model implies more broadly is a commitment towards inter-agency working across a spectrum of health and social care, including building the capacities of community groups. It is underpinned by a radical rethinking and re-evaluation of the fields of mental health and wellbeing informed by substantial and growing research evidence of the potential for social interaction (the 'social cure'), exposure and engagement with nature, mindfulness, engagement with arts and so on. Whether these disparate activities can be coordinated into cohesive programmes offered by health services is open to question and will only become clearer when initiatives such as social prescribing have had some time to grow and develop.

What is clear is that there is a plurality of routes towards mental health and wellbeing that have drawn inspiration from the global movements of people and ideas in this current age of migration. Integration is certainly a challenge requiring organisational change and shifts of resources. At the time of writing there are considerable uncertainties surrounding the economic and political outlook in countries across the globe. There is renewed hostility towards migrants in many parts of the world accompanied by the rise of populist movements. These give rise to countries becoming more unwelcoming and inward looking while promoting a narrow view of valued traditions and cultures. However, a glance back at the movements of peoples and ideas over centuries testifies to the extent to which humans have embraced and adapted ideas and practices from different countries and cultures. The quest for wellbeing and mental health is one in which people have found interconnections between ideas and practices that transcend historical and geographical space and harnessed these for their benefit. In concluding an essay exploring the historical benefits of intercultural engagement, Amartya Sen quotes the renowned poet Rabindranath Tagore, 'Whatever we understand and enjoy in human products instantly becomes ours, wherever they might have their origin' (Sen, 2005, p.86). It may be added that through the various transitions human products undergo in becoming 'ours' we recognise the rich tapestry of intercultural influences that enhance the field of mental health and wellbeing.

Bibliography

Acharyya, S., Moorhouse, S., Kareem, J., & Littlewood, R. (1989). *Nafsiyat: a psychotherapy centre for ethnic minorities. Psychiatric Bulletin*, 13(7), 358–360.

Adam, T. (2011). *Intercultural transfers and the making of the modern world, 1800–2000: sources and contexts.* Macmillan International Higher Education.

Adams, M. & Morgan, J. (2016). An evaluation of a nature- based intervention for people with experiences of psychological distress. Brighton: University of Brighton/Grow.

Agamben, G. (1998). *Homo Sacer: Sovereign Power and Bare Life.* Stanford University Press.

Agamben, G. (2005). *State of Exception.* The University of Chicago Press.

Ager, A., & Strang, A. (2004). *The Experience of Integration: A qualitative study of refugee integration in the local communities of Pollockshaws and Islington.* Research Development and Statistics Directorate, Home Office.

Almedom, A. M. (2005). Social capital and mental health: An interdisciplinary review of primary evidence. *Social science & Medicine, 61(5), 943–964.*

All Party Parliamentary Group (2017). Creative Health: the Arts for Health and Wellbeing. APPG.

Allport, G. W., & Ross, J. M. (1967). Personal religious orientation and prejudice. *Journal of personality and social psychology,* 5(4), 432.

Amarasingham, L. R. (1980). Movement among healers in Sri Lanka: a case study of a Sinhalese patient. *Culture, Medicine and Psychiatry, 4(1), 71–92.*

Amaro, Ajahn (2016). *'I'm Right, You're Wrong'* Attachment to Views, Alienation, and the Buddha's Path of Non-Contention. Amaravati Publications.

Amaro, Ajahn (2017a). *Roots and Currents*: Articles and Essays 1991–2014. Amaravati Publications.

Amaro, Ajahn (2017b). *The Breakthrough*: Buddhist Meditation As A Means Of Liberation. Amaravati Publications.

Ammerman, N. T. (2013). Spiritual but not religious? Beyond binary choices in the study of religion. *Journal for the Scientific Study of Religion,* 52(2), 258–278.

Arendt, H. (1958). *The Human Condition. Second Edition.* The University of Chicago Press.

Aristotle (2004). *The Nicomachean Ethics* Penguin.

Aspinall, P. J., & Watters, C. (2010). *Refugees and asylum seekers: a review from an equality and human rights perspective.* Research Report 52. Equality and Human Rights Commission.

Bachelor, S. (2015). *After Buddhism* Rethinking the *dharma* for a secular age. Yale University Press.

Baggott, R. (2013). *Partnership for Public Health & Wellbeing: Policy and Practice.* Palgrave Macmillan.

Bakhtin, M. (1984). *Problems of Dostoevsky's Poetics* Theory and History of Literature: Vol. 8. Manchester: Manchester University Press.

Basso, K.H. (1996). *Wisdom Sits In Places: Landscape And Among The Western Apache.* University Of New Mexico Press.

Bateson, G. (1962). A note on the double bind. In C. Sluzki & D. Ransom (Eds.). Double bind: The foundation of the commuaicational approach to the family (pp.39–42). New York: Grune &K Stratton.

Bateson, G., Jackson, D., Hdey, J., & Weakland, J. (1956). Toward a theory of schizophrenia. In C. Sluzki & D. Ransom (Eds.), Double bind The foundation of the communicational approach to the family.

Beiser, M. (1999). *Strangers at the gate: The" boat people's" first ten years in Canada*. University of Toronto Press.

Belton, T. (2014). *Happier people, healthier planet*, SilverWood Books.

Berry, J.W. (2011). Integration and multiculturalism: Ways towards social solidarity. *Papers on Social Representations*, 20(1), 2–1.

Berry, J.W., & Sabatier, C. (2010). Acculturation, discrimination, and adaptation among second generation immigrant youth in Montreal and Paris. *International journal of intercultural relations, 34(3),* 191–207.

Berry, J.W., & Sabatier, C.(2011). Variations in the assessment of acculturation attitudes: Their relationships with psychological wellbeing. *International Journal of Intercultural Relations, 35(5), 658–669.*

Berry, J.W. (2008). Globalisation and acculturation. *International Journal of Intercultural Relations, 32(4), 328–336.*

Berry, J.W. (2005). Acculturation: Living successfully in two cultures. *International journal of intercultural relations, 29(6), 697–712.*

Bickerdike, L., Booth, A., Wilson, P. M., Farley, K., & Wright, K. (2017). Social prescribing: less rhetoric and more reality. A systematic review of the evidence. *BMJ open,* 7(4), e013384.

Bishop, R., & Purcell, E. (2013). The value of an allotment group for refugees. *British Journal of Occupational Therapy,76*(6), 264–269.

Bhabha, J., & Crock, M. (2007). Seeking asylum alone: Unaccompanied and separated children and refugee protection in Australia, the UK and the US.

Bowker, J. (1970). *Problems of Suffering in Religion of the World*. Cambridge University Press.

Bourdieu, P. (1986). *The forms of capital.*

Bourdieu, P. et al., (1999). *The Weight of the World: Social Suffering in Contemporary Society*. Polity Press.

Bourdieu, P. (2001). *Homo Academicus*. Polity Press.

Bourdieu, P. (1985). *The social space and the genesis of groups*. Information (International Social Science Council), 24(2), 195–220.

Bourdieu, P & Wacquant, D.J.L. (2007). *An Invitation to Reflexive Sociology*. Polity Press.

Bourdieu, P., & Wacquant, L. (1999). On the cunning of imperialist reason. *Theory, Culture & Society,* 16(1), 41–58.

Brach, T. (2004). *Radical acceptance: Embracing your life with the heart of a Buddha*. Bantam.

BBC (2013). Spiritual, but not Religious by Tom de Castella. *BBC Magazine*. London.

BBC (2018). www.bbc.co.uk/news/world-europe-35250903 (accessed 10th August 2018).

Brown, G. W., & Harris, T. (2012). *Social origins of depression: A study of psychiatric disorders in women.* Routledge.

Brown, R., Baysu, G., Cameron, L., Nigbur, D., Rutland, A., Watters, C., ... & Landau, A. (2013). Acculturation attitudes and social adjustment in British South Asian children: A longitudinal study. *Personality and Social Psychology Bulletin, 39(12), 1656–1667.*

Brown, K.W., & Kasser, T. (2005). *Are psychological and ecological well-being compatible? The role of values, mindfulness, and lifestyle*. Social Indicators Research, 74(2), 349–368.

Carly, J. Wood, Prety, J., Griffin, M.; A case-control study of the health and well-being benefits of allotment gardening, *Journal of Public Health*, Volume 38, Issue 3, 17 September 2016, Pages e336–e344.

Cameron, L., Rutland, A., Douch, R., & Brown, R. (2006). Changing Children's Intergroup Attitudes toward Refugees: Testing Different Models of Extended Contact. *Child Development*, 77(5), 1208–1219.

Cassaniti, J.L. (2018). *Remembering The Present: Mindfulness In Buddhist Asia*. Cornell University Press.

Castells, M. (2000). *The Information Age: Economy, Society and Culture*. End of Millennium 2nd Edition. Blackwell.

Castles, S., & Miller, M.J. (2009). *The Age Of Migration: International Population Movements In The Modern World*. The Guilford Press.

Chiva Giurca, B. (2018). Social prescribing student champion scheme: a novel peer-assisted-learning approach to teaching social prescribing and social determinants of health, *Education for Primary Care*, 29:5, 307–309.

Clark, D.A. (2013). Creating capabilities, lists and thresholds: whose voices, intuitions and value judgements count?. *Journal of Human Development and Capabilities, 14(1), 172–184.*

Codd, R.A. (1999). A critical analysis of the role of Ijtihad in legal reforms in the Muslim world. *Arab law quarterly*, 14(2), 112–131.

Cohen, D. (2006). "Family Constellations": An Innovative Systemic Phenomenological Group Process from Germany. *The Family Journal*. 14. 226–233.

Coleman, J. S. (1988). Social capital in the creation of human capital. *American Journal of Sociology*, 94, S95-S120.

College of Medicine (2018). www.collegeofmedicine.org.uk/dr-michael-dixon-on-radio-4s-today-programme-we-need-to-find-the-right-fit-for-patients-not-just-reach-for-a-pill (accessed 6th July 2019).

Cook, J. (2016). "Mindful in Westminster: The politics of meditation and the limits of neoliberal critique," HAU: *Journal of Ethnographic Theory* 6, no. 1 (Summer 2016): 141–161.

Csordas, T. (2002). *Body, Meaning, Healing*. Springer.

Csordas, T.J. (2007). Introduction: Modalities of transnational transcendence. *Anthropological Theory*, 7(3), 259–272.

Cunsolo Willox, A., Harper, S.L., Ford, J.D., Landman, K., Houle, K., & Edge, V.L. (2012). "From this place and of this place:" climate change, sense of place, and health in Nunatsiavut, Canada. *Social Science & Medicine*, 75(3), 538–547.

Davies, W. (2015). *The happiness industry: How the government and big business sold us wellbeing*. Verso Books.

Dayson, C., & Bashir, N. (2014). The Social and Economic Impact of the Rotherham Social Prescribing Pilot. Centre for Regional Economic and Social Research. Sheffield Hallam University.

Davidson, G., Campbell, J., Shannon, C., & Mulholland, C. (2016). *Models of mental health*. Macmillan International Higher Education.

Derluyn, I., Watters, C., Mels, C., & Broekaert, E. (2012). 'We are All the Same, Coz Exist Only One Earth, Why the BORDER EXIST': Messages of Migrants on their Way. *Journal of Refugee Studies*, 27(1), 1–20.

De Tocqueville, A. (2003). *Democracy in America*. Regnery Publishing.

De Vries, J. (1962). Magic and Religion. *History of Religions, 1*(2), 214–221.

Dickman, N.E. (2016). Linguistically mediated liberation: Freedom and limits of understanding in Thich Nhat Hanh and Hans-Georg Gadamer. *The Humanistic Psychologist*, 44(3), 256.

Dolan, P. (2014). *Happiness by Design: Finding Pleasure and Purpose in Everyday Life*. Penguin.

Dreze, J., & Sen, A. (2002). *India: Development and participation*. Oxford University Press, US.

Drury, J. (2012). 11 Collective resilience in mass emergencies and disasters. The social cure: Identity, health and well-being, 195.

Dudley, M., Silove, D., Gale, F. (2012). *Mental Health and Human Rights: vision, praxis, and courage*. Oxford University Press.

Duncan, W. (2017). Dinámicas Ocultas: Culture and Psy-Sociality in Mexican Family Constellations Therapy. *Ethos, 45*(4), 489–513.

Dunlavy, A., Juárez, S., Toivanen, S., & Rostila, M. (2017). Migration background characteristics and the association between unemployment and suicide. *European Journal of Public Health*, 27(suppl_3).

Eagleton, T. (2008). *Literary Theory: An Introduction*. Blackwell Publishing.

Eck, D. (2011). *India: a sacred geography*. Harmony Books.

Eisenlohr, P. (2012). Cosmopolitanism, globalization, and Islamic piety movements in Mauritius. *City & Society*, *24*(1), 7–28.

EU Observer 15th August 2018

Favell, A. (2001). *Integration policy and integration research in Europe*: A review and critique. In Citizenship today: Global perspectives and practices, Edited by: Aleinikoff, A. and Klusmeyer, D. 349–99. Washington, DC: Brookings Institute/Carnegie Endowment for International Peace.

Fischer, E. (2014). *The Good Life: Aspiration, Dignity, And The Anthropology of Wellbeing*. Stanford University Press.

Frazer, J.G. (1990). *The Golden Bough*. Palgrave Macmillan, London.

Freitas, C. D. (2013). Participation in mental health care by ethnic minority users: Case studies from the Netherlands and Brazil. *REMHU: Revista Interdisciplinar da Mobilidade Humana*, 21(40), 271-272.

Fukuyama, F. (2001). Social capital, civil society and development. *Third world quarlterly*, 22(1), 7–20.

Fernando, S. (2005). *Mental Health Services in the UK*: Lessons from Transcultural Psychiatry in Ingleby, D (Ed) Forced Migration and Mental Health: Rethinking the Care of Refugees and Displaced Persons. Springer. US.

Fernando, S. (2017). *Institutional racism in psychiatry and clinical psychology*. Palgrave Macmillan.

Forest Sangha Newsletter. Summer 2018. Amaravati Publications.

Gallagher, T. (2006). *The Examine Prayer*: Ignition Wisdom for Our Lives Today. Crossroad Publishing.

Glasby, J., & Tew, J. (2015). *Mental health policy and practice*. Macmillan International Higher Education.

Gombrich, R. (1971). *Precept and practice: Traditional Buddhism in the rural highlands of Ceylon*. Oxford University Press.

Gombrich, R. (2012). What the Buddha Thought: An Interview with Richard Gombrich. *Tricycle. Shaheen.*

Gordon B.R., McDowell C.P., Hallgren, M. Meyer, J.D., Lyons, M, Herring, M.P. Association of Efficacy of Resistance Exercise Training With Depressive Symptoms: Meta-analysis and Meta-regression Analysis of Randomized Clinical Trials. *JAMA Psychiatry*. 2018;75(6):566–576.

Gov.UK(2018). www.ethnicity-facts-figures.service.gov.uk/work-pay-and-benefits/pay-and-income/average-hourly-pay/latest (accessed 15th August 2018).

Gov.UK (2019). www.ethnicity-facts-figures.service.gov.uk (accessed 2nd July 2019).

Hansen, M., Jones., R & Tocchini, K. (2017). Shinrin-Yoku (Forest Bathing) and Nature Therapy: A State-of-the-Art Review. *International Journal of Environmental Research and Public Health*.

Hare, M.L. (1993). The emergence of an urban US Chinese medicine. *Medical Anthropology Quarterly*, 7(1), 30–49.

Hargreaves, A. (1995). *Immigration,'race' and ethnicity in contemporary France*. Routledge.

Harpham, T., Grant, E., & Rodriguez, C. (2004). Mental health and social capital in Cali, Colombia. *Social Science & Medicine*, 58(11), 2267–2277.

Harris, N., Minnis, F., & Somerset, S. (2014). Refugees connecting with a new country through community food gardening. *International Journal of Environmental Research and Public Health*, 11(9), 9202–9216.

Harvey, D. (2005). *A Brief History of Neoliberalism*. Oxford University Press.

Harvey, S.B., Øverland, S., Hatch, S.L., Wessely, S., Mykletun, A., & Hotopf, M. (2017). Exercise and the prevention of depression: results of the HUNT cohort study. *Amercian Journal of Psychiatry*, 175(1), 28–36.

Haslam, S.A., Jetten, J., Postmes, T., & Haslam, C. (2009). Social identity, health and well-being: An emerging agenda for applied psychology. *Applied Psychology*, 58(1), 1–23.

Haslam, C., Jetten.J., & Haslam, S.A. (2014). Advancing the Social Cure: Implications for theory, practice and policy in Jetten, J, Haslam, C and Haslam, S.A *The Social Cure: Identity, Healthy and Wellbeing.* Psychology Press

Helman, C.G.(1978). "Feed a cold, starve a fever"—folk models of infection in an English suburban community, and their relation to medical treatment. *Culture, medicine and psychiatry*, 2(2), 107–137.

Hewstone, M. (2015). Consequences of diversity for social cohesion and prejudice: The missing dimension of intergroup contact. *Journal of Social Issues, 71(2), 417–438.*

Hjern, A. (2012). Migration and public health: health in Sweden: the national public health report 2012. *Scandinavian journal of public health, 40(9_suppl), 255–267.*

Holliday, J.S. (2015). *The world rushed in: The California gold rush experience.* University of Oklahoma Press.

Hunger, C., Bornhäuser, A., Link, L., Schweitzer, J., & Weinhold, J. (2014). *Improving experience in personal social systems through family constellation seminars: Results of a randomized controlled trial.* Family Process, 53(2), 288–306.

Huntington, S.P. (1993). *The clash of civilizations?.* Foreign Affairs, 22–49.

Institute of Public Policy Research (2007). *Britain's immigrants: An economic profile,* London: IPPR.

International Conference on Mindfulness (ICM) (2018). www.cmc-im.org

International Organisation for Migration (2018). World Migration Report. IOM. Grand-Saconnex, Switzerland

International Telecommunications Union (2017). *Measuring the Information Society Report* Vol1. Geneva

Ipsos-Mori(2019).www.ipsos.com/ipsos-mori/en-uk/world-apart-brits-have-grown-more-positive-about-immigration (accessed 2nd July 2019).

Irving, A. (2017). *The Art Of Life And Death: Radical Aesthetics and Ethnographic Practice.* Hau Books.

Jacobs, J.L. (1989). The effects of ritual healing on female victims of abuse: A study of empowerment and transformation. *Sociological Analysis*, 50(3), 265–279.

Jaggar, A. M. (2006). Reasoning about well-being: Nussbaum's methods of justifying the capabilities. *Journal of Political Philosophy, 14(3), 301–322.*

James, W. (1985). The Varieties of Religious Experience. Penguin.

Jenkins, H.J. (2015). *Extraordinary Conditions: Culture and Experience in Mental Illness.* University of California Press.

Jetten, J., Haslam, C., & Haslam, S.A. (2014), *The Social Cure: Identity, Health and Wellbeing.* Psychology Press.

Jimenez, A.C. (2008). *Anthropological approaches to Freedom and Political Ethics.* Pluto Press.

Keeley, B. (2007). OECD *Insights Human Capital: How what you know shapes your life.* OECD publishing.

Kyambi, S. (2005). *Beyond black and white: Mapping new immigrant communities.* Institute for Public Policy Research.

Kabat-Zinn, J. (1990). *Full Catastrophe Living: How to cope with stress, pain and illness using mindfulness meditation.* Dell Publishing.

Kareem, J., & Littlewood, R. (2000). *Intercultural therapy.* Blackwell Science.

Keyes, C.L. (2006). Subjective well-being in mental health and human development research worldwide: An introduction. *Social indicators research, 77(1), 1–10.*

King, M., Marston, L., McManus, S., Brugha, T., Meltzer, H., & Bebbington, P. (2013). Religion, spirituality and mental health: results from a national study of English households. *The British Journal of Psychiatry*, 202(1), 68–73.

Kirmayer, J.L. (2012). Culture and Contexts in Human Rights in Dudley,M, Silove,D Gale,F *Mental Health and Human Rights: vision, praxis, and courage*. Oxford University Press.

Kleinman, A. (1980). Patients and healers in the context of culture: An exploration of the borderland between anthropology, medicine, and psychiatry (Vol. 3). *Univ of California Press.*

Kleinman, A. (1988a). *The illness narratives: Suffering, healing and the human condition*. New York: Basic Books.

Kleinman, A. (1988b). *Rethinking Psychiatry: from cultural category to person experience*. The Free Press New York.

Kleinman, A., & Benson, P. (2006). Anthropology in the clinic: the problem of cultural competency and how to fix it. *PLoS medicine, 3*(10), e294.

King, M., Marston, L., McManus, S., Brugha, T., Meltzer, H., & Bebbington, P. (2013). Religion, spirituality and mental health: results from a national study of English households. *The British Journal of Psychiatry, 202*(1), 68–73.

Koenig, H., & Larson, D. (2001). Religion and mental health: Evidence for an association. *International review of psychiatry*, 13(2), 67–78.

Koenig, H.G. (2009). Research on religion, spirituality, and mental health: A review. *The Canadian Journal of Psychiatry, 54*(5), 283–291.

Kohut, H. (2011). *The search for the self*: Selected writings of Heinz Kohut: 1950–1978 (Vol. 4). Karnac Books.

Kyambi, S. (2005). *Beyond black and white – Mapping new immigrant communities*, London: IPPR.

Kreitzer, M.J. (2015). Integrative nursing: Application of principles across clinical settings. *Rambam Maimonides Medical Journal*, 6(2).

Lawrence, E. (1982). Just plain common sense the roots of racism in Centre for Contemporary Cultural Studies eds The Empire strikes back London and New York.

Langer, J.E. (2014). *Mindfulness*: 25th Anniversary Edition. Da Capo Press.

Lautenschlager, N.T., Almeida, O.P., Flicker L. Janca, A. (2004). Can physical activity improve the mental health of older adults? *Ann. Gen. Hosp. Psychiatry*. 2004;3(1):12.

Leff, J. (1988). Psychiatry around the globe: A transcultural view. Gaskell/Royal College of Psychiatrists.

Leff, J. (1973). 'Culture and the Differentiation of Emotional States', *British Journal of Psychiatry*, 125: pp.336–40.

Levi-Strauss, C. (1979). *Structural Anthropology*. Peregrine Books.

Lipowski, Z.J. (1988). Somatization: the concept and its clinical application. *Am. J. Psychiatry*, 145(11), 1358–1368.

Lord, S.A. (2010). *Meditative Dialogue: Cultivating Sacred Space in Psychotherapy–An Intersubjective Fourth?*. Smith College Studies in Social Work, 80(2–3), 269–285.

Luhrmann, T. M. (2013). Making God real and making God good: Some mechanisms through which prayer may contribute to healing. *Transcultural Psychiatry, 50*(5), 707–725.

Lovinger, S.L., Miller, L., & Lovinger, R.J. (1999). Some clinical applications of religious development in adolescence. *Journal of Adolescence*, 22(2), 269–277.

MacIntyre, A. (2007). *After Virtue: Third Edition With New Prologue*. Gerald Duckworth & Co. Ltd.

Meer, N., & Modood, T. (2009). The multicultural state we're in: Muslims,'multiculture'and the 'civic re-balancing'of British multiculturalism. *Political Studies*, 57(3), 473–497.

Meissner, F., & Vertovec, S. (2015). Comparing super-diversity, *Ethnic and Racial Studies, 38:4, 541–555.*

Mayer, C.-H., & Viviers, A. (2016). Constellation work principles, resonance phenomena, and shamanism in South Africa. *South African Journal of Psychology*, 46(1), 130–145.

Michaelson, J. (2013). *Evolving Dharma: Meditation, Buddhism, and the Next Generation of Enlightenment*. North Atlantic Books.

MIND (2018). Nature and Mental Health. *www.mind.org.uk/media/23671047/nature-and-mental-health-2018.pdf*

Mindfulness All-Party Parliamentary Group (2015). Mindful Nation UK. The Mindfulness Initiative, October. www.themindfulnessinitiative.org.uk/images/reports/Mindfulness-APPG-Report_Mindful-Nation-UK_Oct2015.pdf

Modica, M. (2015). Unpacking the 'colorblind approach': accusations of racism at a friendly, mixed-race school. *Race, Ethnicity and Education*, 18(3), pp.396–418.

Modood, T., & May, S. (2001). *Multiculturalism and education in Britain: An internally contested debate. International Journal of Educational Research*, 35(3), 305–317.

Narayanasamy, A., & Owens, J. (2001). A critical incident study of nurses' responses to the spiritual needs of their patients. *Journal of Advanced Nursing*, 33(4), 446–455.

Naslund, J.A., Aschbrenner, K.A., Araya, R., Marsch, L.A., Unützer, J., Patel, V. and Bartels, S.J. (2017). Digital technology for treating and preventing mental disorders in low-income and middle-income countries: a narrative review of the literature. *The Lancet Psychiatry, 4(6), pp.486–500.*

National Health Service (2019). www.nhs.uk/live-well/exercise/guide-to-tai-chi/#what-is-tai-chi (accessed 6th July 2019).

National Health Service (2019). Social Prescribing and Community Based Support. NHS England.

Navsaria, N., & Petersen, S. (2007). *Finding a voice in Shakti: A therapeutic approach for Hindu Indian women. Women & Therapy*, 30(3–4), 161–175.

New Economics Foundation (2018). The Five Ways to Wellbeing: The Evidence. New Economics Foundation. London.

Nierkens, V., Krumeich, A., de Ridder, R., & van Dongen, M. (2002). *The future of intercultural mediation in Belgium.* Patient Education and Counseling, *46(4), 253–259.*

Norcross, J. C., & Goldfried, M. R. (Eds.). (2005). *Handbook of psychotherapy integration.* Oxford University Press.

Nussbaum, M. (2011). *Creating Capabilities: The Human Development Approach.* The Belknap Press Of Harvard University Press.

Obeyesekere, G. (1985). *Depression, Buddhism, and the work of culture in Sri Lanka.* Culture and depression, 134–152.

Ong, A. (2005). *Buddha is Hiding.* University of California Press.

Ong, A. (2016). *Fungible Life: Experiment In The Asian City.* Duke University Press.

Patton, G.C., Coffey, C., Posterino, M., Carlin, J.B., & Bowes, G. (2003). Life events and early onset depression: cause or consequence?. *Psychological Medicine*, 33(7), 1203–1210.

Petty, K.J. (2017). Walking with impaired vision: an anthropology of senses, skill and the environment. Doctoral thesis (PhD), University of Sussex.

Phillips, T. (2005). After 7/7: Sleepwalking to segregation. Website of Commission of Racial Equality.

Pretty, J. (2004). How nature contributes to mental and physical health. *Spirituality and Health International, 5*(2), 68–78.

Pretty, J., Peacock, J., Sellens, M., & Griffin, M. (2005). The mental and physical health outcomes of green exercise. *International journal of environmental health research, 15*(5), 319–337.

Pretty, J., Peacock, J., Sellens, M., & Griffin, M. (2005). The mental and physical health outcomes of green exercise, *International Journal of Environmental Health Research*, 15:5, 319–337

Pretty, J. (2007). *The Earth Only Endures: On Reconnecting With Nature and Our Place In It.* Earthscan.

Pretty, J. (2017). Manifesto for the green mind. *Resurgance & Ecologist,* (301), 18–21.

Pargament, K.I., Magyar-Russell, G.M., & Murray-Swank, N.A. (2005). The sacred and the search for significance: Religion as a unique process. *Journal of social issues,61*(4), 665–687.

Pope Francis (2018). Gaudete Et Exsultate: *On The Call To Holiness In Todays World.* Catholic Truth Society.

Portes, A. (1998). Social capital: Its origins and applications in modern sociology. *Annual Review of Sociology*, 24(1), 1–24.

Prospect Magazine, 20th June, 1998

Prospect Magazine, 29th January 2015

Pun, N., & Chan, J. (2013). The spatial politics of labor in China: Life, labor, and a new generation of migrant workers. *South Atlantic Quarterly*, 112(1), 179–190.

Purser, R., & Loy, D. (2013). Beyond McMindfulness. *Huffington post*, 1(7), 13.

Ronald, E., Purser, R. (2018). Critical perspectives on corporate mindfulness, *Journal of Management, Spirituality & Religion*, 15:2, 105–108

Putnam, R.D. (2001). *Bowling alone: The collapse and revival of American community*. Simon and Schuster.

Putnam, P., Robert, 'E Pluribus Unum: Diversity and Community in the Twenty-First Century: The 2006 Johan Skytte Prize Lecture', *Scandinavian Political Studies*, 30 (2007), 137–174

Rack, P. (1982). *Race, Culture and Mental Disorder* (London: Tavistock).

Rapport, N. J. (2006). "*In Praise of Displacement*: 'In Order to' Motives, and Existential Power". In R. Fletcher (Ed.), Beyond Resistance: The Future of Freedom (pp.123–142). Nova Science.

Rober, P., & De Haene, L. (2014). Intercultural therapy and the limitations of a cultural competency framework: About cultural differences, universalities and the unresolvable tensions between them. *Journal of Family Therapy*, 36, 3–20.

Roe, C. A., Sonnex, C., & Roxburgh, E.C. (2015). Two meta-analyses of noncontact healing studies. *Explore*, 11(1), 11–23.

Rose, N (2018) *Our Psychiatric Future*. Polity Press.

Rose, V.K., & Thompson, L.M. (2012). Space, place and people: a community development approach to mental health promotion in a disadvantaged community. *Community Development Journal*, 47(4), 604–611.

Rothon, C., Goodwin, L., & Stansfeld, S. (2012). Family social support, community "social capital" and adolescents' mental health and educational outcomes: a longitudinal study in England. *Social Psychiatry and Psychiatric Epidemiology*, 47(5), 697–709.

Royal College of General Practitioners (2017). Spotlight on the 10 High Impact Actions. Royal College of GPs. London

Ruiz-Casares, C., Rousseau, C., Derluyn, I., Watters, C., & Crépeau, F. (2012). Right and access to healthcare for undocumented children: addressing the gap between international conventions and disparate implementations in North America and Europe. *Social Science & Medicine*, 70(2), 329–336.

Rutland, A., Cameron, L., Jugert, P., Nigbur, D., Brown, R., Watters, C., & Le Touze, D. (2012). Group identity and peer relations: A longitudinal study of group identity, perceived peer acceptance, and friendships amongst ethnic minority English children. *British Journal of Developmental Psychology, 30(2)*, 283–302.

Ryff, C.D., & Keyes, C.L.M. (1995). The structure of psychological well-being revisited. *Journal of personality and social psychology*, 69(4), 719.

Said, E. (2001). The Clash of Ignorance. *The Nation*, 22.

Sartorius, N. (2003). Social capital and mental health. *Current Opinion in Psychiatry, 16*, S101-S105.

Scarry, E. (1985). *The Body In Pain: The Making and Unmaking of the World*. Oxford University Press.

Scruton, R. (2012). Green Philosophy: *How To Think Seriously About The Planet*. Atlantic Books.

Seikkula, J., & Olson, M.E. (2003). The open dialogue approach to acute psychosis: Its poetics and micropolitics. *Family process, 42*(3), 403–418.

Seikkula, J., & Trimble, D. (2005). *Healing elements of therapeutic conversation: Dialogue as an embodiment of love. Family process*, 44(4), 461–475.

Seikkula, J. (2002). Monologue is the crisis- Dialogue becomes the aim of therapy. *Journal of Marital and Family Therapy*, 28(3), 283–284.

Seikkula, J., Alakare, B., Aaltonen, J., Holma, J., Rasinkangas, A., & Lehtinen, V. (2003). Open dialogue approach: Treatment principles and preliminary results of a two-year follow-up on first episode schizophrenia. *Ethical Human Sciences and Services*, 5(3), 163–182.

Sen, A. (1999). *Development as Freedom*. New York: Alfred A. Knopf.

Sen, A. (2005). *The Argumentative Indian: Writing on Indian Culture, History and Identity*. Penguin Group.

Sen, A. (2007). *Identity & Violence: The Illusion of Destiny*. Penguin Books.

Sennett., R. (2013). *Together: The Rituals, Pleasures & Politics Of Cooperation*. Penguin Group.

Sheldrake, R. Schützenberger, A. A., & Hellinger, B. (2000). Re-viewing assumptions: a dialog about phenomena that challenge our word-view. Carl-Auer-Systeme-Verlag.

Shimmin, P., Watters, C., Osborn, D. (2018). Open spaces for health: concluding report Sussex Community Development Association

Shinn, M. (2015). Community psychology and the capabilities approach. *American journal of community psychology*, 55(3–4), 243–252.

Silove, D., Steel, Z., McGorry, P., & Dobny, J. (1999). Problems Tamil asylum seekers encounter in accessing health and welfare services in Australia. *Social Science and Medicine*, 49, 951–956.

Silove, D., Steel, Z., & Watters, C. (2000). Policies of deterrence and the mental health of asylum seekers. *Journal of the American Medical Association, 284(5), 604–611.*

Skultans, V. (2007). *Empathy and healing: Essays in Medical and Narrative Anthropology*. Berghahn Books.

Skultans, V. (1987). The management of mental illness among Maharashtrian families: a case study of a Mahanubhav healing temple. *Man*, 661–679.

Smart, N. (1981). *Beyond Ideology: Religion and the Future of Western Civilisation*. Collins.

Söderbäck, M., Coyne, I, & Harder, M. (2011). The importance of including both a child perspective and the child's perspective within health care settings to provide truly child-centred care. *Journal of Child Health Care*, 15(2), pp.99–106.

Stiefel, I., Harris, P., & Zollmann, A.W. (2002). Family Constellation—A Therapy Beyond Words. *Australian and New Zealand Journal of Family Therapy*, 23(1), 38–44.

Sternberg, E. (2009). *Healing Places: The Science of Place and Well Being*. The Belknap Press of Harvard University Press.

Sturgis, P., Brunton-Smith, I., Read, S., & Allum, N. (2011). Does Ethnic Diversity Erode Trust? Putnam's 'Hunkering Down' Thesis Reconsidered. *British Journal of Political Science*, 41(1), 57–82.

Sumedho, Ajahn. (2014). *Peace is a Simple Step*. Amaravati Publications.

Tambiah, S.J. (1977). *World Conqueror & World Renouncer: A Study of Buddhism and Polity in Thailand against a Historical Background*. Cambridge University Press.

Tambiah, S.J. (1970). *Buddhism and the spirit cults in north-east Thailand*. Cambridge University Press.

Tausch, N., Saguy, T., & Bryson, J. (2015). How does intergroup contact affect social change? Its impact on collective action and individual mobility intentions among members of a disadvantaged group. *Journal of Social Issues*, 71(3), 536–553.

Taussig, M (1987) *Shamanism, Colonialism and the Wild Man: A Study in Terror and Healing*. University of Chicago Press.

Taussig, M.T. (1982). *The devil and commodity fetishism in South America*. University of North Carolina Press.

Teasdale, J., Zindel, V., Segal, J., Williams, M., Ridgeway, V., Soulsby, J., & Lau, M. (2000). Prevention of relapse/recurrence in major depression by mindfulness-based cognitive therapy. *Journal of Consulting and Clinical Psychology* 68: 615–23.

De Tocqueville, A. (2003). *Democracy in America*. Regnery Publishing.

Thanissara (2015). Time to Stand Up: An Engaged Buddhist Manifesto for Our Earth. North Atlantic Books.

Thornicroft, G., Ahuja, S., Barber, S., Chisholm, D., Collins, P. Y., Docrat, S., ... & Patel, V. (2018). Integrated care for people with long-term mental and physical health conditions in low-income and middle-income countries. *The Lancet Psychiatry*.

The Guardian 18th August 2018

The Guardian 28th August 2018

The Times 18th August 2018

The Times 30th August 2018

Trani, J.F., & Bakhshi, P. (2017). A multidimensional approach to poverty: implications for global mental health. In *The Palgrave Handbook of Sociocultural Perspectives on Global Mental Health* (pp.403–428). Palgrave Macmillan, London.

Trimble, D. (2002). Listening with integrity: The dialogical stance of Jaakko Seikkula. *Journal of Marital and Family Therapy*, 28(3), 275–277.

Turner, R.N., & Brown, R. (2008). Improving Children's Attitudes Toward Refugees: An Evaluation of a School-Based Multicultural Curriculum and an Anti-Racist Intervention. *Journal of Applied Social Psychology*, 38(5), 1295–1328.

UNHCR (2018). The State of the World's Refugees. United Nations High Commission for Refugees. Geneva.

Waley, A. (2013). *The way and its power: A study of the Tao Te Ching and its place in Chinese thought*. Routledge.

Watters, C. (1996). *Representations of Asians' mental health in British psychiatry. In The social construction of social policy* (pp.88–105). Palgrave Macmillan, London.

Watters. C (2008). *Refugee Children: Towards the Next Horizon*. Routledge.

Watters, C., Hossain, R., Brown, R., & Rutland, A. (2009). Crossing thresholds: acculturation and social capital in British Asian children. In *Theorizing identities and social action* (pp.198–219). Palgrave Macmillan, London.

Watters, C. (2001). *Emerging paradigms in the mental health care of refugees*. Social Science & Medicine, 52(11), 1709–1718.

Watters, C., & Ingleby, D. (2004). International Locations of care: Meeting the mental health and social care needs of refugees in Europe. *Journal of Law and Psychiatry, 27(6),* 549–570.

Watters, C. (2002). *Migration and mental health care in Europe: report of a preliminary mapping excercise*.

Watters, C. (2007). *Refugee children: Towards the next horizon*. Routledge.

Watters, C., Hossain, R., Brown, R. and Rutland, A., (2009). *Crossing thresholds: Acculturation and social capital in British Asian children*. In Theorizing identities and social action (pp.198–219). Palgrave Macmillan, London.

Watters, C (2012) Mental Health and Illness as Human Rights Issues in Dudley, M., Silove, D., & Gale, F. (Eds.) *Mental health and human rights: vision, praxis, and courage*. Oxford University Press.

Watters, C. (2001). *Emerging paradigms in the mental health care of refugees. Social Science & Medicine, 52*(11), 1709–1718.

Wetherell, M. (2009). *Identity in the 21st Century: New Trends in Changing Times*. Palgrave Macmillan.

White, R. G., Imperiale, M.G., & Perera, E. (2016). The Capabilities Approach: Fostering contexts for enhancing mental health and wellbeing across the globe. *Globalization and Health, 12(1),* 16.

White, S., & Abeyasekera, A. (2014). *Wellbeing and quality of life assessment: a practical guide*. Practical Action Publishing.

Whiten, A., Caldwell, C., & Masoudi, A. (2016). Cultural Diffusion in Humans and Other Animals. *Current opinion in Psychology. Vol 8 p15–21.* Elsevier

Wilkinson, R., & Pickett, K. (2010). *The spirit level: Why equality is better for everyone*. Penguin UK.

Willox, A.C., Harper, S.L., Ford, J.D., Edge, V.L., Landman, K., Houle, K., ... & Wolfrey, C. (2013). Climate change and mental health: an exploratory case study from Rigolet, Nunatsiavut, Canada. *Climatic Change*, 121(2), 255–270.

Williams, M., & Penman, D. (2011). *Mindfulness: a practical guide to finding peace in a frantic world*. Piatkuz.

Williams, R. (2014). *Being Christian: Baptism, Bible, Eucharist, Prayer*. Society of Christian Knowledge.

Wong, L.T., Mui, K.W., & Hui, P.S. (2006). A statistical model for characterizing common air pollutants in air-conditioned offices. *Atmospheric Environment*, 40(23), 4246–4257.

Wong, V.C.N. (2009). Use of complementary and alternative medicine (CAM) in autism spectrum disorder (ASD): comparison of Chinese and western culture (Part A). *Journal of Autism and Developmental Disorders*, 39(3), 454–463.

Wood, C.J., Pretty, J., & Griffin, M. (2016). A case–control study of the health and well-being benefits of allotment gardening. *Journal of Public Health*, 38(3), e336–e344.

World Health Organization (2013). Mental Health Action Plan. WHO, Geneva

Yarris, R.K. (2017). *Care Across Generations: Solidary and Sacrifice in Transnational Families*. Stanford University Press.

Yeary, K.H.C.K., Ounpraseuth, S., Moore, P., Bursac, Z., & Greene, P. (2012). Religion, social capital, and health. *Review of Religious Research*, 54(3), 331–347.

Yu, C.P., Lin, C.M., Tsai, Y.C., Chen, C.Y. (2017). Effects of Short Forest Bathing Program on Autonomic Nervous System Activity and Mood States in Middle-Aged and Elderly Individuals. *International Journal of Environmental Research and Public Health*. 2017;14(8):897.

Zhang, X., Zhang, X., & Chen, X. (2017). Happiness in the air: How does a dirty sky affect mental health and subjective well-being? *Journal of Environmental Economics and Management*, 85, 81–94.

Index

Lightning Source UK Ltd.
Milton Keynes UK
UKHW020215140222
398641UK00004B/130